Introduction

When I started freesciencelessons in 2013, I had one simple
their understanding of science. When I was at school (and we're talking thirty years ago now), science was always my favourite subject. It's not surprising that I went on to become a science teacher. I know that many students find science challenging. But I really believe that this doesn't have to be the case. With patient teaching and a bit of hard work, any student can make amazing progress.

Back in 2013, I had no idea how big freesciencelessons would become. The channel now has nearly 70 million views from 192 countries with a total view time of over 300 years. I love to hear from the students who have patiently watched the videos and realised that they can do science after all, despite in many cases having little confidence in their ability. And just like in 2013, I still make all the videos myself (many students think that I have a staff of helpers, but no, it's just me).

This workbook is designed to complement the Physics 1 videos for the AQA specification. However, there is a huge amount of overlap with other exam boards and in the future I'll be making videos and workbooks for those as well. I've packed the workbook full of questions to help you with your science learning. You might decide to start at the beginning and answer every question in the book or you might prefer to dip in and out of chapters depending on what you want to learn. Either way is fine. I've also written very detailed answers for every question, again to help you really develop your understanding. You can find these by scanning the QR code on the front of the book or by visiting freesciencelessons.co.uk/p1tv1

Please don't think of science as some sort of impossible mountain to climb. Yes there are some challenging bits but it's not as difficult as people think. Take your time, work hard and believe in yourself. When you find a topic difficult, don't give up. Just go to a different topic and come back to it later.

Finally, if you have any feedback on the workbooks, you're welcome to let me know (support@freesciencelessons.co.uk). I'm always keen to make the workbooks better so if you have a suggestion, I'd love to hear it.

Good luck on your journey. I hope that you get the grades that you want.

Shaun Donnelly

Revision Tips

The first important point about revision is that you need to be realistic about the amount of work that you need to do. Essentially you have to learn two years of work (or three if you start GCSEs in Year 9). That's a lot of stuff to learn. So give yourself plenty of time. If you're very serious about getting a top grade then I would recommend starting your revision as early as you can. I see a lot of messages on Youtube and Twitter from students who leave their revision until the last minute. That's their choice but I don't think it's a good way to get the best grades.

To revise successfully for any subject (but I believe particularly for science), you have to really get into it. You have to get your mind deep into the subject. That's because science has some difficult concepts that require thought and concentration. So you're right in the middle of that challenging topic and your phone pings. Your friend has sent you a message about something that he saw on Netflix. You reply and start revising again. Another message appears. This is from a different friend who has a meme they want to share. And so on and so on.

What I'm trying to tell you is that successful revision requires isolation. You need to shut yourself away from distractions and that includes your phone. Nothing that any of your friends have to say is so critically important that it cannot wait until you have finished. Just because your friends are bored does not mean that your revision has to suffer. Again, it's about you taking control.

Remember to give yourself breaks every now and then. You'll know when it's time. I don't agree with people who say you need a break every fifteen minutes (or whatever). Everyone is different and you might find that your work is going so well that you don't need a break. In that case don't take one. If you're taking breaks every ten minutes then the question I would ask is do you need them? Or are you trying to avoid work?

There are many different ways to revise and you have to find what works for you. I believe that active revision is the most effective. I know that many students like to copy out detailed notes (often from my videos). Personally, I don't believe that this is a great way to revise since it's not really active. A better way is to watch a video and then try to answer the questions from this book. If you can't, then you might want to watch the video again (or look carefully at the answers to check the part that you struggled with).

The human brain learns by repetition. So the more times that you go over a concept, the more fixed it will become in your brain. That's why revision needs so much time because you really need to go over everything more than once (ideally several times) before the exam.

Revision Tips

I find with my students that flashcards are a great way to learn facts. Again, that's because the brain learns by repetition. My students write a question on one side and the answer on the other. They then practise them until they've memorised the answer. I always advise them to start by memorising five cards and then gradually adding in extra cards, rather than try to memorise fifty cards at once.

I've noticed over the last few years that more students do past paper practise as a way of revising. I do not recommend this at all. A past paper is what you do AFTER you have revised. Imagine that you are trying to learn to play the guitar. So you buy a guitar and rather than having lessons, you book yourself into a concert hall to give a performance. And you keep giving performances until you can play. Would you recommend that as a good strategy? I wouldn't. But essentially that's how lots of students try to revise. Yes by all means do practise papers (I've included a specimen paper in this book for you) but do them at the end when you've done all your revision. Past papers require you to pull lots of different bits of the specification together, so you should only do them when you are capable of that (ie when you've already done loads of revision).

A couple of final points ....

To reduce our environmental impact and to keep the price of this book reasonable, the answers are available online. Simply scan the QR code on the front or visit www.freesciencelessons.co.uk/p1tv1

There will be times when I decide to update a book, for example to make something clearer or maybe to correct a problem (I hope not many of those). So please keep an eye out for updates. I'll post them on Twitter (@UKscienceguy) and also on the FAQ page of my website. If you think that you've spotted a mistake or a problem, please feel free to contact me.

Physics Equation Sheet

Word Equation	Symbol Equation	Higher Only
elastic potential energy = 0.5 x spring constant x (extension)²	$E_e = \frac{1}{2} k e^2$	
change in thermal energy = mass x specific heat capacity x temperature change	$\Delta E = m c \Delta\theta$	
thermal energy for a change of state = mass x specific latent heat	$E = m L$	
For gases: pressure x volume = constant	$p V = \text{constant}$	
pressure due to a column of liquid = height of column x density of liquid x gravitational field strength (g)	$p = h \rho g$	Yes
(final velocity)² - (initial velocity)² = 2 x acceleration x distance	$v^2 - u^2 = 2as$	
force = change in momentum / time taken	$F = \frac{m\Delta v}{\Delta t}$	Yes
period = 1 / frequency	$T = \frac{1}{f}$	
magnification = image height / object height		
force on a conductor (at right angles to a magnetic field) carrying a current = magnetic flux density x current x length	$F = B I l$	Yes
potential difference across primary coil / potential difference across secondary coil = number of turns in primary coil / number of turns in secondary coil	$\frac{V_p}{V_s} = \frac{n_p}{n_s}$	Yes
potential difference across primary coil x current in primary coil = potential difference across secondary coil x current in secondary coil	$V_p I_p = V_s I_s$	Yes

4

Significant Figures

Significant figures are easier than you might think. There are a few rules to learn but once you've got the hang of them, they're quite straightforward.

Non-zero numbers

All numbers which are not zero are significant.

For example, the number 453 has three significant figures.

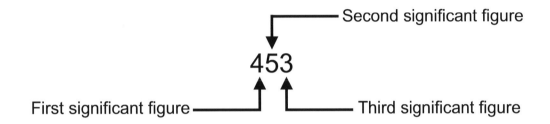

Dealing with zeros.

We can class zeros into three different types.

<u>Zeros between two non-zero numbers</u>

• Zeros between two non-zero numbers are always significant.

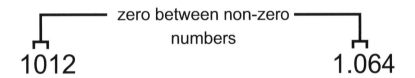

Both of these numbers have four significant figures. That's because in both cases, the zero is between two non-zero numbers and is significant.

Question 1 - State the number of significant figures in the following:

1128   478.2   201   1.109

Zeros before the first non-zero number

- These are called leading zeros.

- Leading zeros are not significant.

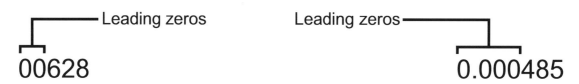

Both of these numbers have three significant figures. That's because the leading zeros are not significant.

Question 2 - State the number of significant figures in the following:

0.04115   00.79   0123   005.6

Zeros after the last non-zero number

- These are called trailing zeros.

- If a number has a decimal point, then trailing zeros are significant.

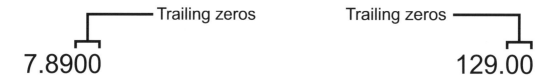

Both of the above numbers have five significant figures. That's because the trailing zeros are after a decimal point and are significant.

- If a number does not have a decimal point, then trailing zeros are generally not significant. This is not always true but for GCSE science, it probably is.

In this case, both of the above numbers have three significant figures. That's because there is no decimal point so the trailing zeros are not significant.

In your GCSE exams, you could be expected to round numbers to a certain number of significant figures. The questions on the following page will help you.

Question 3. Round the following numbers to the significant figures shown.

a. Round 3.0682 to three significant figures.

b. Round 120.14 to four significant figures.

c. Round 0.005673 to two significant figures.

d. Round 0.1025 to three significant figures.

e. Round 215.6714 to four significant figures.

Contents

Contents

Contents

Contents

Chapter 1: Energy

- Describe what is meant by kinetic energy and calculate the kinetic energy of moving objects.

- Describe what is meant by gravitational potential energy and calculate the gravitational potential energy of an object raised above the ground.

- Describe what is meant by elastic potential energy and calculate the elastic potential energy of a stretched or compressed object eg a spring.

- Use the idea of specific heat capacity to calculate the energy required or released when an object changes temperature.

- Describe what is meant by the law of conservation of energy.

- Describe the energy transfers taking place when a pendulum swings and explain why a pendulum eventually stops swinging.

- Describe the energy transfers taking place during a bungee jump and explain why a bungee jumper cannot bounce back to their starting position.

- Calculate the work done by a force in moving an object.

- Calculate the power of an energy transfer.

- Calculate the efficiency of an energy transfer.

- Describe what is meant by thermal conductivity.

- Describe the factors that determine how quickly a building cools.

- Describe how to determine the specific heat capacity of a material (required practical).

- Describe how to determine the effectiveness of materials as thermal insulators (required practical).

- Describe the advantages and disadvantages of fossil fuels as a source of energy.

- Describe the advantages and disadvantages of nuclear power as a source of energy.

- Explain why the UK needs to use a range of different energy sources.

- Describe what is meant by a renewable energy resource.

- Describe examples of renewable energy resources and discuss their advantages and disadvantages.

Kinetic Energy

$$\text{kinetic energy (J)} = 0.5 \times \text{mass (kg)} \times \text{speed}^2 \text{ (m/s)}$$

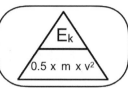

1. Calculate the kinetic energy store of the following objects.

a. A ball with a mass of 0.5 kg moving with a speed of 10 m/s.

$\frac{1}{2}mv^2$

$\frac{1}{2} \times 0.5 \times 10^2 = 25$

Kinetic energy = __25__ J

b. A boy on a scooter travelling at 2.5 m/s. The combined mass of the boy and scooter is 30 kg.

$\frac{1}{2} \times 30 \times 2.5^2 = 93.75$

Kinetic energy = __93.75__ J

2. a. A car with a mass of 800 kg is travelling at 15 m/s. Calculate the kinetic energy store in kJ.

$\frac{1}{2} \times 800 \times 15^2 = 90000 = 90kj$

Kinetic energy = __90__ kJ

b. The car now doubles in speed to 30 m/s. What will happen to the kinetic energy store?

| The kinetic energy store will double | The kinetic energy store will halve | The kinetic energy store will increase by four times ✓ |

Explain your answer.

3. Calculate the mass of the following objects.

a. A mouse is moving with a speed of 0.1 m/s and has a kinetic energy store of 0.0001 J.

$$\frac{1}{2}v \quad m = \frac{E_k}{0.5 \times v^2}$$

$$= \frac{0.0001}{0.5 \times 0.1^2} = 0.02$$

Mass = __0.02__ kg

b. A dog is moving with a speed of 90 cm/s and has a kinetic energy store of 12 J.

Give your answer to 3 significant figures.

$$m = \frac{12}{0.5 \times 0.9^2}$$

$$= 0.00296$$

$$= 29.6$$

Mass = __29.6__ kg

4. Calculate the speed of the following objects.

a. A biker and motorbike have a combined mass of 230 kg and a kinetic energy store of 46 kJ.

$$v^2 = \frac{46000}{0.5 \times 230}$$

$$v = \sqrt{ANS}$$

$$= 20$$

Speed = __20__ m/s

b. A rugby ball has a mass of 450 g and a kinetic energy store of 38 J.

Give your answer to 2 significant figures.

$$v^2 = \frac{38}{0.5 \times 0.45}$$

$$v = \sqrt{ANS}$$

$$= 13$$

Speed = __13__ m/s

Gravitational Potential Energy

Exam tip: You are not given this equation in the exam.

gravitational potential energy (J) = mass (kg) x gravitational field strength (N/kg) x height (m)

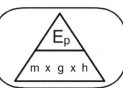

1. What is meant by the gravitational potential energy store?

The energy stored in an object due to its position above the Earth's surface. force due to gravity acting on the object.

2. Calculate the change in the gravitational potential energy store of the following objects.

a. A cat with a mass of 3 kg climbs a tree, reaching a final height of 4.5 m (g = 9.8 N/kg).

$3 \times 4.5 \times 9.8 = 132.3$

Change in gravitational potential energy store = _____132.3_____ J

b. A book with a mass of 950 g is placed on a shelf which is 1.5 m above the ground (g = 9.8 N/kg).
Give your answer to 4 significant figures.

Change in gravitational potential energy store = _____ J

c. A bag with a mass of 4.5 kg is placed on a table which is 75 cm above the ground (g = 9.8 N/kg).
Give your answer to 2 significant figures.

Change in gravitational potential energy store = _____ J

3. A window cleaner climbs a ladder, to a final height of 3 m above the ground. The change in the gravitational potential energy store of the window cleaner is 2000 J. Calculate the mass of the window cleaner (g = 9.8 N/kg).

4. Calculate the height reached by the following objects.

a. A climber with a mass of 75 kg is climbing a cliff-face. At the top of the cliff, her gravitational potential energy store is 14 700 J (g = 9.8 N/kg).

Height = _____ m

b. A helicopter with passengers has a mass of 1400 kg. The gravitational potential energy store is 2 700 kJ (g = 9.8 N/kg).

Give your answer to 4 significant figures.

Height = _____ m

5. The Mars rover has a mass of 185 kg. The rover climbed a hill on Mars, reaching a final height of 8 m. The gravitational potential energy store of the rover was 5476 J.

Calculate the value of the gravitational field strength on Mars.

g = _____ N / kg

6. A roller-coaster car has a total mass of 1000 kg. At the top of the roller-coaster, the car is at a height of 60 m.

a. Calculate the gravitational potential energy store of the car at the top of the roller-coaster (g = 9.8 N/kg).

b. Calculate the maximum speed of the car when it reaches the bottom of the roller-coaster. You can assume that all of the gravitational potential energy store has been converted to the kinetic energy store.

Give your answer to 3 significant figures.

c. Suggest why the actual speed of the roller-coaster car will be less than the value you calculated in part b.

Elastic Potential Energy

Exam tip: You are given this equation in the exam but not the units.

$$\text{elastic potential energy (J)} = 0.5 \times \text{spring constant (N/m)} \times \text{extension (m)}^2$$

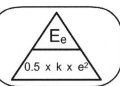

1. What is meant by the elastic potential energy store?

2. A scientist applied a force to a spring and measured the extension as she gradually increased the force. The graph is shown below.

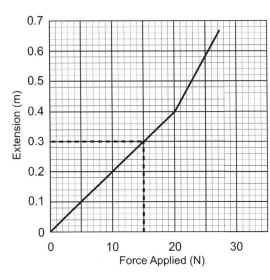

a. Explain how the graph shows that the extension is directly proportional to the force applied.

b. Use the graph to determine the extension when a force of 15 N is applied to the spring.

c. Label the section of the graph which shows that the limit of proportionality has been exceeded.

d. Which of the following statements is correct (circle the correct answer)?

Exceeding the limit of proportionality, the spring extends more for the force applied

Exceeding the limit of proportionality, the spring extends less for the force applied

Exceeding the limit of proportionality, the spring extends the same for the force applied

e. The spring constant can be determined using the following equation:

$$\text{spring constant (N/m)} = \frac{\text{change in force applied (N)}}{\text{change in extension of spring (m)}}$$

Exam tip: You do not need to learn this equation

Use the graph to determine the spring constant of the spring.

3. a. A spring has a spring constant of 15 N/m. The spring is extended by 0.2 m.

Calculate the elastic potential energy store of the spring.

Elastic potential energy store =_____ J

3. b. A spring has a spring constant of 50 N/m. The original length of the spring is 25 cm. The spring is extended so that the final length is 50 cm.

Calculate the elastic potential energy store of the spring. Give your answer to 3 significant figures.

Elastic potential energy store =_____ J

4. A spring is extended by 0.12 m. The elastic potential energy store of the spring is 0.144 J.

Calculate the spring constant of the spring.

Spring constant =_____ N / m

5. a. A spring has a spring constant of 100 N/m. The spring is extended so that the elastic potential energy store of the spring is 5 J.

Calculate the extension of the spring. Give your answer to 2 significant figures.

Extension =_____ m

5. b. Beyond this extension, much less force was required to extend the spring further. Suggest what may have happened to the spring at this point.

Specific Heat Capacity

1. An electric kettle is used to increase the temperature of 0.6 kg of water by 80°C.

Calculate the thermal energy store of the water (specific heat capacity of water = 4200 J/kg °C).

Thermal energy store = _____ kJ

2. An oil-filled radiator contains 10 kg of oil. The starting temperature of the radiator was 20°C and the final temperature was 65°C.

Calculate the thermal energy store of the radiator (specific heat capacity of oil = 1800 J/kg °C).

Thermal energy store = _____ kJ

3. A cup of coffee cools down from 75°C to 20°C. Calculate the thermal energy transferred from the coffee to the surroundings. The mass of the coffee was 300 g and the specific heat capacity of water is 4200 J/kg °C.

Energy transferred = _____ kJ

4. A block of aluminium has a starting temperature of 25°C. 136.5 kJ of thermal energy are transferred into the block raising the temperature to 75°C.

Calculate the mass of the aluminium block. The specific heat capacity of aluminium is 910 J/kg °C.

Mass = _____ kg

5. The mass of air in a room is 367 kg. An electric heater transfers 3692 kJ of thermal energy into the air. The temperature of the air increases from 10°C to 20°C.

Calculate the specific heat capacity of air. Give your answer to 4 significant figures.

Specific Heat Capacity = _____ J/kg °C

6. A bottle of water is placed in a warm room. The starting temperature of the water is 5°C and the mass of the water is 330 g. 20.79 kJ of thermal energy transfers into the water.

Calculate the final temperature of the water. The specific heat capacity of water is 4200 J/kg °C.

Final temperature = _____ °C

Energy Transfers: Pendulum

1. What is meant by the Law of Conservation of Energy?

2. The diagram below shows a pendulum swinging in air.

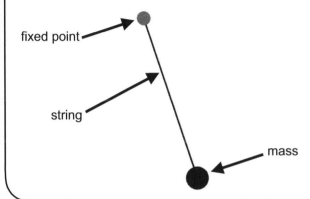

fixed point

string

mass

a. State the different parts of this system.

b. This is a closed system. What is meant by a closed system?

3. The diagram shows the pendulum at different stages in its swing.

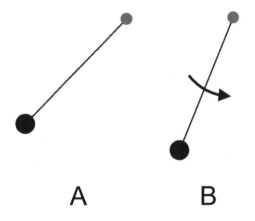   

A   B   C   D   E

Link each stage in the pendulum swing to the correct statement below.

At this stage, the gravitational potential energy store is being transferred to the kinetic energy store.

 A

 B

 C

At this stage, the pendulum is moving at its maximum speed. The kinetic energy store is maximum but the gravitational potential energy store is zero.

At this stage, the kinetic energy store is being transferred to the gravitational potential energy store.

 D

 E

At this stage, the pendulum is not moving. The kinetic energy store is zero. The gravitational potential energy store is maximum.

4. The diagram below shows how the position of the pendulum changes with time.

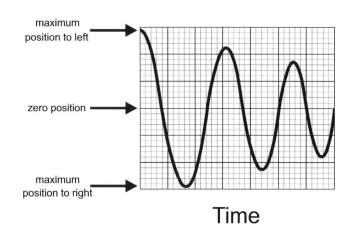

maximum position to left

zero position

maximum position to right

Time

a. On the diagram, label the following parts.

- Where the kinetic energy store is at its maximum.
- Where the gravitational potential energy store is at its maximum.
- Where the kinetic energy store is at its minimum.
- Where the gravitational potential energy store is at its minimum.

b. Explain why the maximum positions to the left and right reduce for each swing of the pendulum.

c. State two ways that we can reduce this effect.

5. A pendulum has a mass of 1 kg. The mass is swung to a vertical height of 0.5 m and released.

a. Calculate the gravitational potential energy store of the pendulum at its maximum height (g = 9.8 N/kg).

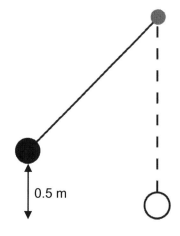

0.5 m

b. Assuming that all of the gravitational potential energy store is converted to the kinetic energy store, state the maximum kinetic energy store of the pendulum.

c. Using your answer to part b, calculate the maximum speed the pendulum mass reaches during its swing.

Give your answer to 2 significant figures.

Energy Transfers: Bungee Jumper

Exam tip: A bungee jumper is a good example of energy transfers so don't be surprised to see a question on this in your exam.

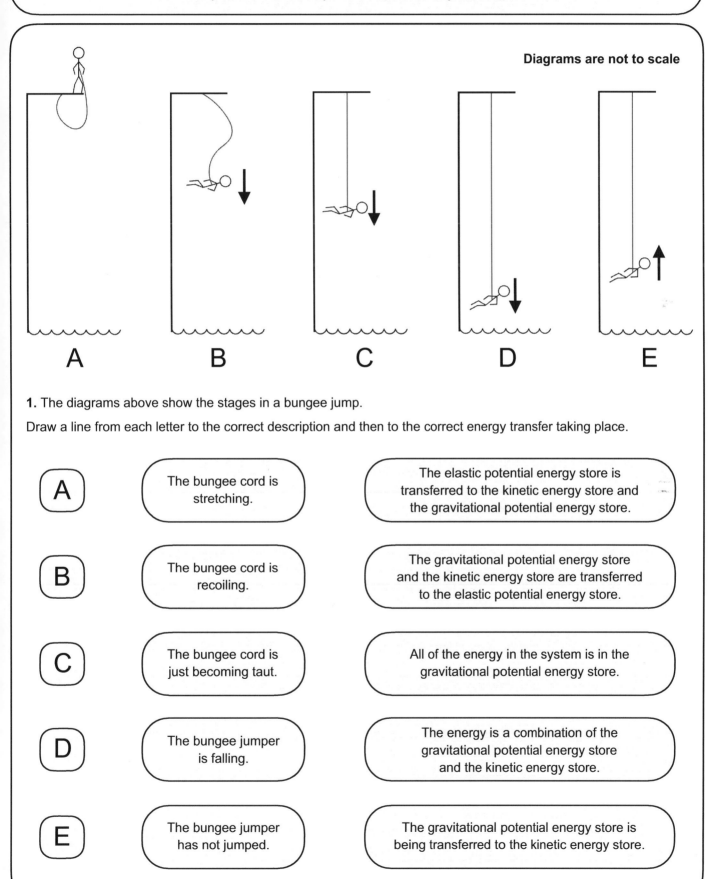

Diagrams are not to scale

A   B   C   D   E

1. The diagrams above show the stages in a bungee jump.

Draw a line from each letter to the correct description and then to the correct energy transfer taking place.

A	The bungee cord is stretching.	The elastic potential energy store is transferred to the kinetic energy store and the gravitational potential energy store.
B	The bungee cord is recoiling.	The gravitational potential energy store and the kinetic energy store are transferred to the elastic potential energy store.
C	The bungee cord is just becoming taut.	All of the energy in the system is in the gravitational potential energy store.
D	The bungee jumper is falling.	The energy is a combination of the gravitational potential energy store and the kinetic energy store.
E	The bungee jumper has not jumped.	The gravitational potential energy store is being transferred to the kinetic energy store.

2. The diagrams below show a closer look at the first part of the bungee jump. The distance fallen at the point where the bungee cord just starts to become taut is 15 m. The mass of the jumper is 80 kg.

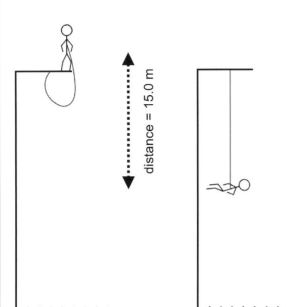

a. Calculate the change in the gravitational potential energy store of the jumper from the starting position to the point where the cord just becomes taut (g = 9.8 N/kg).

b. State the kinetic energy store of the jumper after falling a distance of 15 m (assume that all of the gravitational potential energy store has been transferred to the kinetic energy store).

c. From your answer to part b, calculate the speed of the jumper after they have fallen a distance of 15 m.

Give your answer to 3 significant figures.

3. At the lowest point of the fall, the bungee cord has an extension of 15 m greater than the unstretched length.

a. The spring constant of the bungee cord is 60 N/m. Calculate the elastic potential energy store of the stretched bungee cord. You will need to use the equation for elastic potential energy from page 17.

b. Describe two reasons why the energy stored in the fully-stretched bungee cord will be less than the gravitational potential energy store of the jumper before they have jumped.

Work Done by a Force

$$\text{work done (J)} = \text{force (N)} \times \text{distance moved along the line of action of the force (m)}$$

W
F x s

---

1. A go kart is travelling around a circuit. The driver applies a force of 100 N to the brakes and the go cart comes to a stop in 4 m.

a. State the energy transfers taking place as the go kart comes to a stop.

b. Calculate the work done in bringing the go kart to a stop.

Work done = _____ J

---

2. A force of 3750 N is applied by the engine of a van to accelerate the van from a stationary position over a distance of 20 m.

a. State the energy transfers taking place as the van accelerates.

b. Calculate the work done in accelerating the van.

Work done = _____ J

---

3. A toy car comes to a stop over a distance of 40 cm. A force of 0.3 N was required to bring the car to a stop.

Calculate the work done in stopping the toy car.

Work done = _____ J

4. A car comes to a stop in 20 m. The work done to stop the car is 140 000 J.

Calculate the force required to bring the car to a stop.

Force = _____ N

5. A person pushes a box along the ground. The force required to push the box is 40 N and the work done is 200 J.

Calculate the distance that the box was pushed.

Distance = _____ m

6. A crane lifts an object with a mass of 50 kg a vertical distance of 20 m.

a. Calculate the change in the gravitational potential energy store of the object (g = 9.8 N/kg).

Change in gravitational potential energy store = _____ J

b. Calculate the force applied by the crane to lift the object. Assume that the work done is the same as the change in the gravitational potential energy store.

Force = _____ N

Calculating Power

$$\text{power (W)} = \frac{\text{energy transferred (J)}}{\text{time (s)}}$$

Exam tip: You are not given these equations in the exam.

$$\text{power (W)} = \frac{\text{work done (J)}}{\text{time (s)}}$$

1. What is meant by "power"?

2. Calculate the power of the following energy transfers.

a. A lamp transfers a total of 1800 J of energy into light in 120 seconds.

Power = _____ W

b. A hairdryer transfers a total of 288 000 J of energy into thermal energy and kinetic energy in 480 seconds.

Power = _____ W

c. A kettle transfers a total of 360 000 J of energy into thermal energy in 3 minutes.

Power = _____ W

3. Calculate the power of the following energy transfers.

a. A pick-up truck uses a winch to lift a car. A total of 15 000 J of work is done in 2 minutes.

Power = _____ W

b. A cyclist accelerates their bicycle from a stopped position. The total work done is 1000 J and the time taken is 16 seconds.

Power = _____ W

4. An oven has a power of 2000 W and is used for 10 minutes.

Calculate the total energy transferred by the oven during this time.

Energy transferred = _____ J

5. A man lifts a box up a flight of stairs. The work done is 980 J and the power of the man is 50 W.

Calculate the time taken to lift the box.

Time taken = _____ s

Efficiency

$$\text{efficiency} = \frac{\text{useful output energy transfer}}{\text{total input energy transfer}}$$

Exam tip: You are not given these equations in the exam.

$$\text{efficiency} = \frac{\text{useful power output}}{\text{total power input}}$$

1. Complete the following paragraph using the words below.

created   useful   greater   fraction

The efficiency of an energy transfer tells us what _____ of the energy we put into

an appliance is transferred to _____ forms of energy. We can never get an efficiency

_____ than 100%. This would mean that we had _____ energy.

2. Calculate the efficiency of the following energy transfers.

a. A Bunsen burner is used to heat water. The Bunsen burner transfers 500 J of chemical energy to thermal energy. 200 J of the thermal energy passes into the water.

Efficiency = _____

b. A motor is used to lift an object. 5000 J of energy is transferred by the motor. The gravitational potential energy store of the object increases by 4000 J.

Efficiency = _____

3. Calculate the efficiency of the following energy transfers.

a. A TV has a power of 150 W. 130 W are transferred to light and 5 W are transferred to sound.

Efficiency = _____ %

b. A LED bulb has a power of 8 W. 7 W are transferred to light and 1 W is transferred to thermal energy.

Efficiency = _____ %

Exam tip: Remember that efficiency must either be calculated as a decimal or a percentage. Do not mix these up in your final answer.

4. A games console has a power of 200 W and an efficiency of 0.9.

Calculate the useful power output.

Useful power output = _____ W

5. A computer has an efficiency of 0.8. The useful power output of the computer was 160 W.

Calculate the total power input.

Total power input = _____ W

6. The diagrams below show electric hobs being used to heat two different pans of water.

Arrows show the transfer of thermal energy.

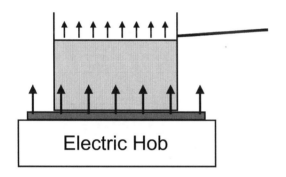

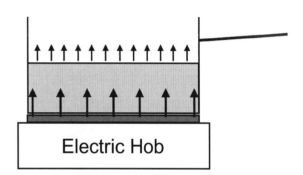

a. Which of these two pans is the most efficient for heating water? Explain your answer.

b. Explain how using a lid would make both pans more efficient.

c. The kettle shown on the right has plastic walls. Suggest three reasons why using a kettle is more efficient for heating water than using a pan.

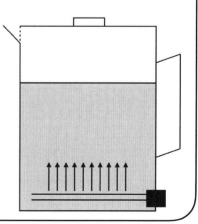

Cooling of Buildings

1. The diagram below shows the walls of a house in the UK.

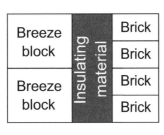

Interior of house | Exterior of house

a. The insulating material between the breeze blocks and the bricks has a very low thermal conductivity.

What is meant by a low thermal conductivity?

b. Explain the advantage of packing the cavity with insulating material in houses in the UK.

2. Many houses in the UK have double-glazed windows and loft insulation.

Single-glazed and double-glazed windows are shown below.

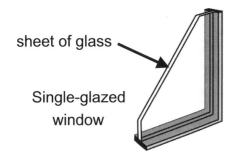

Single-glazed window

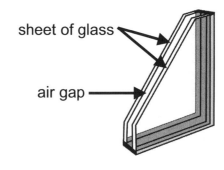

Double-glazed window

a. Glass has a thermal conductivity of 5.8 and air has a thermal conductivity of 3.7.

Explain how double-glazing reduces thermal energy transfer from a house to the outside.

b. Describe how loft insulation reduces thermal energy transfer through the roof of a house.

3. Apart from using insulating materials, what other way can we reduce the rate of thermal energy transfer from a house?

Required Practical: Specific Heat Capacity

1. In this practical, we are going to determine the specific heat capacity of a material. In this example, we are going to use a liquid such as oil or water.

a. We start by placing an empty beaker onto a balance and setting the balance to zero.

Sometimes we get a reading on the balance even when it should read zero. Scientists call this zero error. A zero error is caused by a faulty balance and cannot be reduced by doing repeats.

What type of error is zero error? Circle the correct box.

Random error

Systematic error

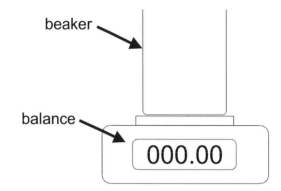

b. We now pour our liquid into the beaker and record the mass of the liquid.

If we know that our balance has a zero error then we need to correct for this.

If our balance has a zero error of 5g and a final mass reading of 800g, what is the actual mass of our liquid?

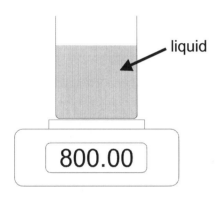

c. Next we place an immersion heater and thermometer into the liquid. We now record the starting temperature of the liquid. Different students can read the same piece of equipment and get different results. This can lead to random errors. Random errors do not depend on the equipment.

Explain why reading the temperature on the thermometer can lead to random errors.

d. How can we reduce the effect of random errors?

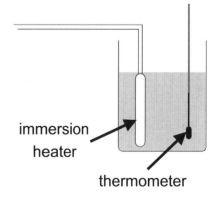

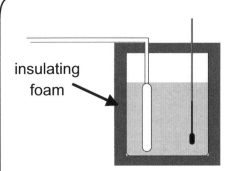

insulating foam

2. Next we wrap the beaker in insulating foam.

Explain the importance of this step.

3. We now connect the immersion heater to a joulemeter and a power pack.

Explain the function of the joulemeter.

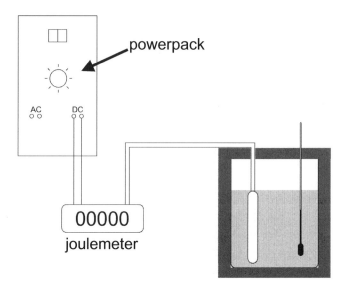

powerpack

AC

DC

00000
joulemeter

At this point, we turn on the powerpack and leave the apparatus for around 10-30 minutes (depending on the material). This will give enough time for the temperature of the liquid to increase.

4. Finally, we read the final temperature on the thermometer and the total number of joules of energy transferred to thermal energy by the immersion heater. We can then use these to calculate the specific heat capacity of the liquid.

A beaker contains 800 g of a liquid. The initial temperature of the liquid was 20°C and the final temperature was 68°C. A total of 75212 J of energy passed into the immersion heater.

Use the equation below to calculate the specific heat capacity of the liquid. Give your answer to 5 significant figures.

$$\text{specific heat capacity (J/kg °C)} = \frac{\text{change in thermal energy (J)}}{\text{mass (kg)} \times \text{temperature change (°C)}}$$

Exam tip: The equation involving specific heat capacity is given in the exam so you do not need to learn it. However, the units are not given.

5. As well as doing the practical with a joulemeter, we can also use a slightly different method.

In this case, we use an ammeter and a voltmeter. A diagram of this is shown on the right.

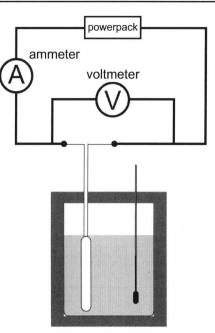

To calculate the energy that passes into the immersion heater, we read the current from the ammeter and the potential difference from the voltmeter. **You will see much more about these in chapter 2 "Electricity".**

The power is calculated using the following equation:

power (W)   =   potential difference (V)   x   current (A)

As we saw on page 27, we calculate the energy as follows:

energy (J)   =   power (W)   x   time (s)

A beaker contained 1.2 kg of liquid. This was heated using an immersion heater for 60 minutes. The potential difference across the immersion heater was 60 V and the current was 0.3 A.

The starting temperature of the liquid was 20°C and the final temperature was 80°C.

Calculate the specific heat capacity of the liquid.

$$\text{specific heat capacity (J/kg °C)} \quad = \quad \frac{\text{change in thermal energy (J)}}{\text{mass (kg)} \ \times \ \text{temperature change (°C)}}$$

6. There are four main sources of inaccuracy with this practical. These are shown below.

Describe a way to reduce each source of inaccuracy.

Source of inaccuracy	Solution
Thermal energy passing out of the beaker into the air	
Not all thermal energy passing into the oil	
Incorrect reading of the thermometer	
Thermal energy not being spread through the oil	

Required Practical: Thermal Insulators

Exam tip: This required practical is straightforward. Focus on getting the ideas of independent variable, dependent variable and control variables.

1. In the first part, we compare the effectiveness of different materials as thermal insulators.

We start by placing a small beaker inside a larger beaker. We then transfer 80 cm³ of water into the central beaker. This water should be hot (for example 80°C).

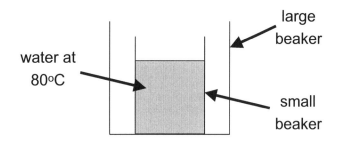

water at 80°C · large beaker · small beaker

Exam tip: Remember that you do not need to learn exact measurements such as the temperature and volume of the water. In the exam, you can suggest your own values.

a. Explain why we need to use a measuring cylinder to measure the volume of water rather than simply using the beaker.

b. Complete the sentence by circling the correct box.

Both the volume and starting temperature of the water are kept the same. We call these ...

(Independent variables)   (Control variables)   (Dependent variables)

c. We then cover the beaker with a lid and measure the starting temperature of the water using a thermometer. Finally, we start a stop watch.

Explain the purpose of the lid.

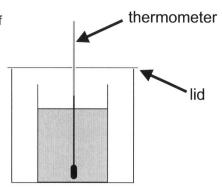

thermometer · lid

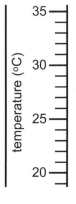

d. The diagram on the left shows a section of a thermometer.

State the resolution of this thermometer and explain your answer.

We now use the thermometer to measure the temperature of the water every three minutes for fifteen minutes.

Next, we repeat the experiment but this time we fill the gap between the two beakers with an insulating material for example bubble wrap or cotton wool.

insulating
material

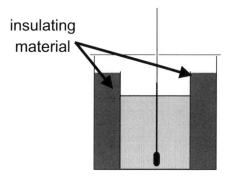

2. Any experiment has an independent variable (IV), a dependent variable (DV) and control variables (CV).

a. Write the definition of these variables in the spaces below.

Independent variable (IV)	Dependent variable (DV)	Control variables (CV)

b. Tick the correct box to show which category the following variables fall into.

	Independent variable	Dependent variable	Control variable
Mass of insulating material	☐	☐	☐
Starting temperature of water	☐	☐	☐
Volume of water	☐	☐	☐
Type of insulating material	☐	☐	☐
Temperature change	☐	☐	☐
Sizes of the beakers	☐	☐	☐
Temperature of the surroundings	☐	☐	☐

3. A student investigated two different insulating materials. The results of their experiment are shown in the graph below. The table shows the thermal conductivity of the two materials. We saw thermal conductivity in the topic on "Cooling of Buildings" on page 32.

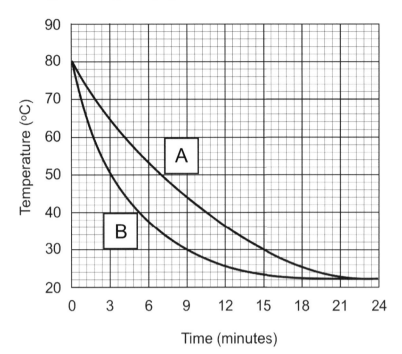

Material	Thermal Conductivity (arbitrary units)
Cork	0.070
Polystyrene	0.033

Exam tip: You might see "arbitrary units" in your exam. Don't worry about this. It just means that the units are not important to the question so they have not included them.

a. Using the table and the graph, identify which of the two materials are cork and polystyrene.

Cork = material _____

Polystyrene = material _____

Explain your answer using data from the graph.

b. Use the graph to determine the temperature of the room.

Room temperature = _____ ºC

c. The rate of cooling can be determined using the equation below (you do not need to know this equation).

Calculate the rate of cooling using material A between 3 minutes and 12 minutes.

Give your answer to 3 significant figures.

$$\text{rate of cooling (ºC / minute)} = \frac{\text{change in temperature (ºC)}}{\text{time (minutes)}}$$

Rate of cooling = _____ ºC / minute

4. Another experiment on thermal insulators is shown below.

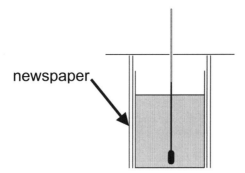

newspaper

We start with 80 cm³ of hot water in a beaker. We now measure the temperature of the water every three minutes for fifteen minutes.

Now we wrap the beaker in two layers of newspaper and repeat the experiment.

We now carry out the experiment again using four layers of newspaper and then six layers.

State the independent variable, dependent variable and control variables in this experiment.

Independent variable (IV)	Dependent variable (DV)	Control variables (CV)

5. A student's results for 2 sheets of newspaper are shown below.

a. Plot the student's results on the graph paper and draw a line of best fit.

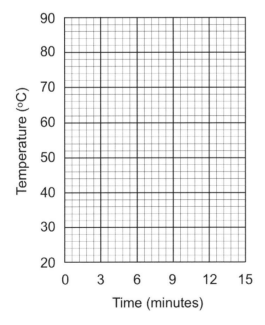

Time (minutes)	Temperature (°C)
0	80
3	60
6	42
9	20
12	26
15	24

b. Identify the anomalous result on the graph and state a possible reason for this result.

Energy from Fossil Fuels

1. The list below shows a number of different sources of energy.

Circle the sources of energy that are fossil fuels.

(Nuclear power)   (Gas)   (Solar power)   (Wind power)

(Oil)   (Hydroelectric)   (Coal)   (Biomass)

2. Fossil fuels have a number of advantages. Complete the following paragraph using the words below.

cheap   airplanes   renewable   versatile   energy   abundant   reliable

Fossil fuels are _____ because they are always available to provide energy (unlike

_____ energy sources). Fossil fuels can also release a very large amount of

_____ which makes them useful for example for _____ . Fossil fuels

are also _____ (ie there are large amounts in the world). This also makes them relatively

_____ . Lastly, fossil fuels are _____ and can be used for transport,

heating and generating electricity.

3. Fossil fuels also have a number of disadvantages.

a. Burning fossil fuels releases carbon dioxide. Why is this a problem?

b. Fossil fuels are non-renewable. What is the definition of non-renewable?

c. Burning diesel and coal releases other pollutants. Link the fuel to the pollutant and then to the problem with that pollutant.

(Diesel)

(Sulfur dioxide)

(Carbon particles)

(Coal)

(Nitrogen oxides)

(These can increase the risk of breathing disorders and heart disease)

(This can cause acid rain, damaging buildings and trees)

Nuclear Power

1. Nuclear power plants generate electricity by using two different elements.

a. State the two elements that can be used to generate electricity in a nuclear power plant.

b. The elements used in nuclear power plants are not being replenished (replaced) as we use them.

What do scientists call resources which are not replenished as they are used?

2. Generating electricity using nuclear power has a number of advantages and disadvantages.

Next to each statement below, write A for an advantage and D for a disadvantage.

Because a nuclear power plant contains radioactive elements, at the end of its life, it must be carefully dismantled. This is called decommissioning and this takes many years and is very expensive.

Once a nuclear power plant has been built, generating electricity produces no carbon dioxide. This means that nuclear power does not contribute to climate change.

Nuclear power plants contain a large amount of highly radioactive elements. These are potentially extremely dangerous if they are ever released eg due to an accident or natural disaster.

Nuclear power plants generate radioactive waste. This is highly dangerous and must be safely stored for many thousands of years before it is safe.

A nuclear power plant will always generate a lot of electricity exactly when it is needed. This means that nuclear power is extremely reliable.

3. State the main advantage of generating electricity using nuclear power compared to burning fossil fuels.

The UK Energy Mix

1. In the 1950s, almost all of the heating and electricity in the UK was generated by burning coal.

a. Which of the following explains why coal was used so extensively at the time?

> The UK had to import all of the coal it used and this made it expensive

> The UK has large deposits of coal so it was extremely cheap and easy to get

> Scientists thought that burning coal was leading to climate change

b. Two developments took place which meant that coal use dropped sharply.

State the two developments in the space below.

c. Generating electricity by burning gas has several advantages compared to burning coal.

Complete the following paragraph using the words below.

coal   **switched on**   **carbon dioxide**   **climate change**   **start-up**

Generating electricity by burning gas generates less _____ than burning coal.

This means that burning gas contributes less to _____ . Gas-fired power stations can

also be _____ very rapidly when demand for electricity is high. This is called a short

_____ time. _____ power stations have a very long start-up time.

2. In the 1970s, scientists began to suspect that burning fossil fuels contributes to climate change.

a. Fossil fuels were still used extensively to provide energy in the UK. This is due to economic factors. Explain what is meant by economic factors.

b. Describe a disadvantage of using wind power to generate electricity.

c. In the future, renewables will provide most of our electricity along with nuclear and gas-fired power stations. Describe the role of the nuclear power stations and gas-fired power stations in this system.

Nuclear power stations	Gas-fired power stations

Renewable Sources of Energy

1. There are many different types of renewable energy resources.

Which of the following are the two advantages shared by **all** renewable energy resources?

| They are cheap | They will never run out | They generate a lot of electricity | They do not release carbon dioxide |

2. Wind power and solar power are used to generate a lot of electricity in the UK.

Explain why we cannot rely on solar power or wind power to provide **all** of the UK's electricity.

3. Hydroelectric power is used to generate electricity in many parts of the world.

a. Describe one advantage and one disadvantage of using hydroelectric power to generate electricity.

b. Explain why hydroelectric power is not used very much in the UK.

4. Tidal power, wave power and geothermal power could be used to generate electricity in the UK.

Describe the main advantage of these methods of generating electricity.

5. Biofuels could be used to power vehicles such as cars or buses.

a. Biofuels are carbon neutral. Explain what this means.

b. What is the main problem of using biofuels as a source of renewable energy?

Chapter 2: Electricity

- Recognise and use component symbols used in electrical circuits.

- Describe what is meant by an electrical current and how this is measured.

- Describe how the path of an electrical current is different in series and parallel circuits.

- Describe what is meant by potential difference and how this is measured.

- Describe how potential difference varies in series and parallel circuits.

- Calculate the potential difference produced by batteries.

- Calculate the charge flowing around a circuit.

- Calculate the energy transferred by components in a circuit.

- Calculate the resistance of components in a circuit.

- Calculate the resistance of a resistor and describe what is meant by an ohmic conductor.

- Describe how the resistance of a filament lamp changes with the potential difference.

- Describe how the resistance of a diode changes with the potential difference.

- Describe the function of a light-emitting diode (LED).

- Calculate the total resistance of resistors in series and describe the resistance of resistors in parallel.

- Describe how the resistance of a light-dependent resistor (LDR) changes with light intensity and describe uses of an LDR.

- Describe how the resistance of a thermistor changes with temperature and describe uses of a thermistor.

- Describe how to investigate how the resistance of a wire depends on the length of the wire (required practical).

- Describe how to investigate how the current running through a component depends on the potential difference across the component (required practical).

- Calculate the energy transferred by an appliance.

Chapter 2: Electricity

- Calculate the power of a component given the current and potential difference or calculate the current or potential difference when given the power.

- State the difference between a DC and an AC power supply.

- Use an oscilloscope trace to determine whether a power supply is DC or AC and to determine the frequency (of an AC supply) and potential difference.

- Describe the functions of the live, neutral and earth wires in a power cable.

- Explain how a fuse protects users from electrocution by an electrical appliance.

- Describe what is meant by the National Grid and explain how the National Grid reduces energy losses in electrical transmission.

- Explain how objects can become charged by static electricity.

- Describe what is meant by an electric field and use the idea of an electric field to explain the force of attraction or repulsion between two charged objects.

Current in Series Circuits

1. The diagram below shows four symbols for components found in electrical circuits.

Under each symbol, write the name of the component.

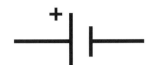

Name = _____

Name = _____

Name = _____

Name = _____

2. The diagram on the right shows a simple series circuit.

a. Explain what is meant by a series circuit.

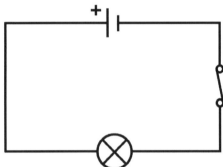

b. When the switch is closed, an electrical current flows around the circuit.

What is meant by an electrical current?

c. Explain why the electrical current causes the filament lamp to light up.

d. Draw an arrow to show the conventional current on the circuit diagram above.

Exam tip: Remember that the conventional current is an old-fashioned idea that is still used in Physics. In all of the diagrams in this topic, the arrow shows the conventional current.

3. Electrical current is a flow of charge around a circuit.

a. We measure electrical current using an ammeter. Draw the symbol for an ammeter in the space below.

b. Which of the following shows the unit for electrical current?

volt (V)   ampere (A)   ohm (Ω)

c. The diagram below shows two lamps in series.

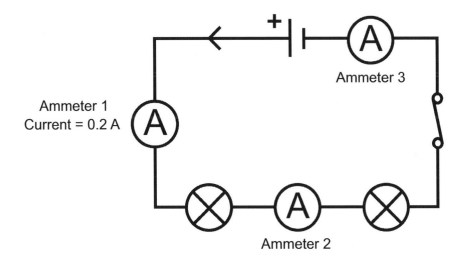

Ammeter 3

Ammeter 1
Current = 0.2 A

Ammeter 2

State the current shown by the ammeters in the circuit and explain your answer.

Ammeter 2 = _____ A   Ammeter 3 = _____ A

Explanation:

d. A student says "Current falls around a circuit as it is used up by the lamps".

Explain why the student's statement is incorrect.

Current in Parallel Circuits

1. The diagrams below show a circuit with two bulbs in series and a circuit with two bulbs in parallel.

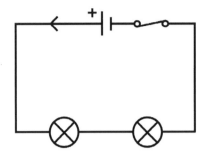

Two bulbs in series

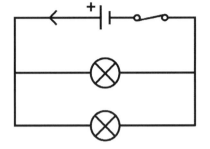

Two bulbs in parallel

a. Describe two differences between a parallel circuit and a series circuit.

b. Calculate the current shown by the ammeters in the parallel circuits below.

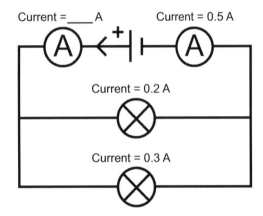

Current = ____ A
Current = 0.5 A
Current = 0.2 A
Current = 0.3 A

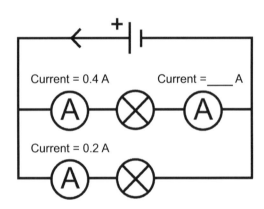

Current = 0.4 A
Current = ____ A
Current = 0.2 A

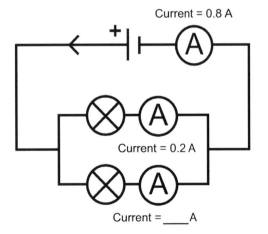

Current = 0.8 A
Current = 0.2 A
Current = ____ A

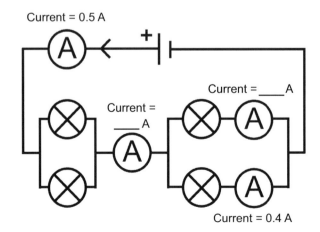

Current = 0.5 A
Current = ____ A
Current = ____ A
Current = 0.4 A

Potential Difference in Series Circuits

1. Complete the following paragraph using the words below.

transferred   **chemical**   **potential**   **thermal**   **electrons**

The cell has a store of _____ energy. The energy is carried around the circuit by

_____. When the electrons pass through components, some of the energy is

_____ to other forms of energy for example light and _____ energy.

The _____ difference across a component gives us an idea of the energy

transferred by that component.

2. The diagram shows a simple circuit.

a. Complete the diagram to show the potential difference across the lamp.

b. Explain your answer to part a.

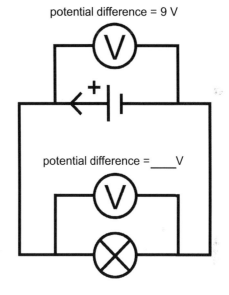

potential difference = 9 V

potential difference = ____V

c. Another identical lamp was added in series with the first lamp. The diagram of this circuit is shown on the right.

Complete the diagram to show the potential difference across the two lamps.

d. Explain why the two lamps in the bottom circuit will both be less bright than the single lamp in the top circuit.

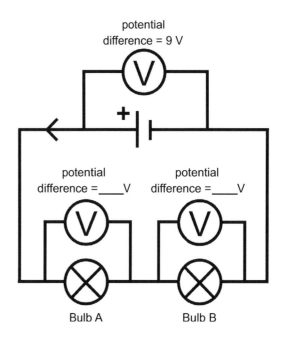

potential difference = 9 V

potential difference = ____V   potential difference = ____V

Bulb A   Bulb B

3. The diagram shows a circuit with two lamps in series. These two lamps are not identical.

a. Complete the diagram to show the potential difference across lamp B.

b. Which lamp will be brighter?

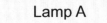 Lamp A   Lamp B

c. Explain your answer to part b.

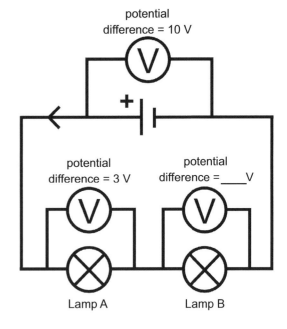

potential difference = 10 V

potential difference = 3 V   potential difference = ___ V

Lamp A   Lamp B

---

4. These circuits each contain one mistake. Describe the mistake for each circuit and describe how to correct it.

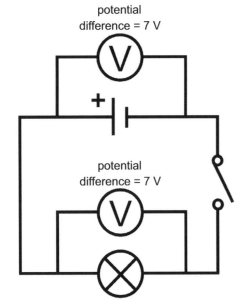

potential difference = 7 V

potential difference = 7 V

Mistake:

How to correct mistake:

Mistake:

How to correct mistake:

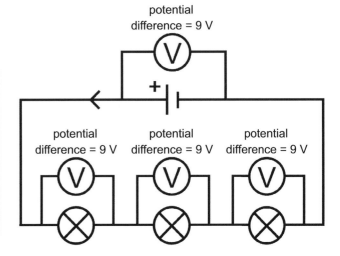

potential difference = 9 V

potential difference = 9 V   potential difference = 9 V   potential difference = 9 V

Potential Difference in Parallel Circuits

1. The diagram on the right shows a simple parallel circuit containing two identical lamps.

a. Complete the diagram to show the potential difference across the two lamps.

b. Using your answer to part a, compare the brightness of the two lamps.

c. Explain your answer to part b.

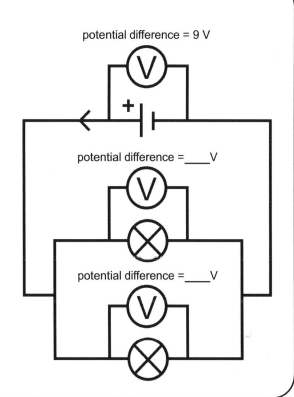

potential difference = 9 V

potential difference =____V

potential difference =____V

2. The diagram on the right shows a circuit containing three lamps: A, B and C.

a. Complete the diagram to show the potential difference across the lamp in the top branch and the cell.

b. Which lamp will be brightest?

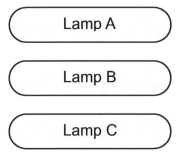

Lamp A

Lamp B

Lamp C

c. Explain your answer to part b.

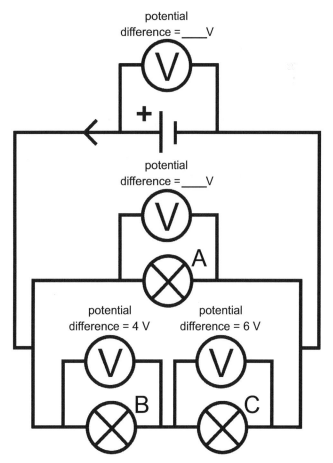

potential difference =____V

potential difference =____V

potential difference = 4 V

potential difference = 6 V

A

B

C

Potential Difference from Batteries

1. Electrical circuits often contain batteries. A battery is two or more cells connected together.

Draw the symbol for a battery in the space below.

2. Calculate the overall potential difference of the batteries below.

Assume that each cell has a potential difference of 4 V.

a.

potential difference = ____ V

b.

potential difference = ____ V

c.

potential difference = ____ V

d.

potential difference = ____ V

3. Calculate the potential differences below. Assume that each cell has a potential difference of 4 V.

a.

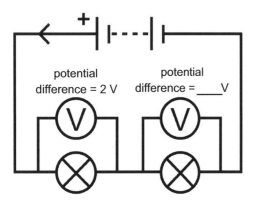

potential difference = 2 V   potential difference = ____ V

b.

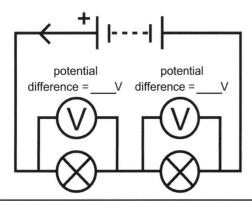

potential difference = ____ V   potential difference = ____ V

4. Calculate the potential difference of each cell in the battery below. Explain your answer.

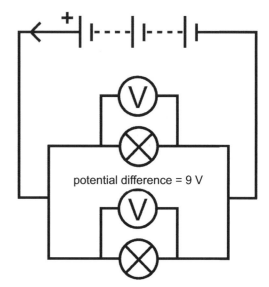

potential difference = 9 V

Explanation:

Charge in Circuits

Exam tip: You are not given this equation in the exam.

charge flow (C)   =   current (A)   x   time (s)

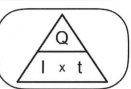

1. The diagram on the right shows a series circuit.

a. Calculate the total charge flowing through the circuit in 15 s.

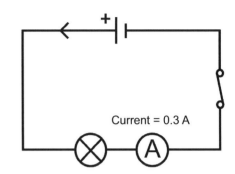

Current = 0.3 A

b. A total charge of 150 C flowed through the circuit.

Calculate the time that the current was flowing.

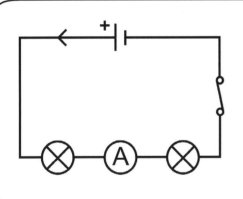

2. A total charge of 75 C flowed through the circuit on the left. The time taken was 150 s.

Calculate the current reading on the ammeter.

3. The diagram on the right shows a parallel circuit.

a. A total charge of 20 C flowed through the bottom branch in 80 s. Calculate the current in the bottom branch.

b. Using your answer to a, determine the current returning to the cell.

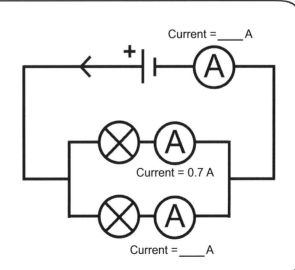

Current = _____ A

Current = 0.7 A

Current = _____ A

Calculating Energy Transfer by Components

energy transferred (J) = charge flow (C) x potential difference (V)

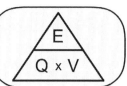

1. The diagram on the right shows a lamp connected to a cell.

a. A total of 1.5 C of charge passes through the lamp. Calculate the energy transferred by the lamp during this time.

b. Using the idea of energy transfer, explain why the potential difference across the cell must be the same as the potential difference across the lamp.

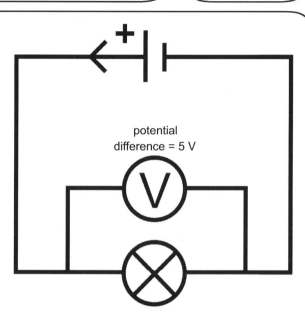

potential difference = 5 V

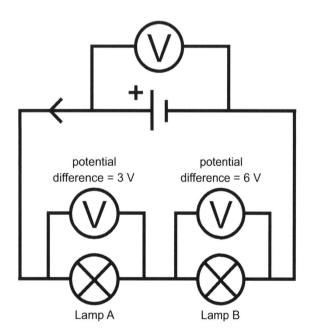

potential difference = 3 V

potential difference = 6 V

Lamp A

Lamp B

2. The diagram on the left shows two lamps connected in series.

a. A total of 4 C of charge passes through the circuit. Calculate the energy transferred by lamp A and by lamp B.

b. From your answer to part a, calculate the total energy transfer of the circuit.

c. From your answer to part b, show that the potential difference across the cell must be 9 V.

In a previous video, we saw that components connected in parallel have the same potential difference as the cell. Students often wonder how the electrons can provide the same energy to two different branches. The question below shows you how.

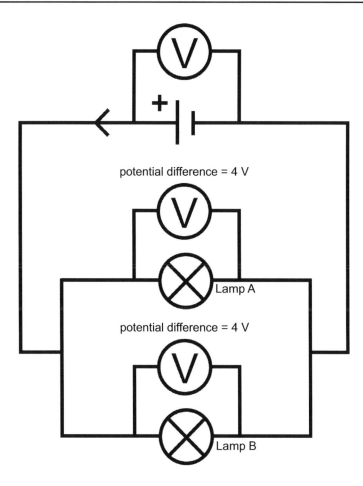

potential difference = 4 V

Lamp A

potential difference = 4 V

Lamp B

3. The diagram above shows two identical lamps connected in parallel.

a. A total of 4 C of charge passes through lamp A. Calculate the energy transferred by the lamp during this time.

b. A total of 4 C of charge also passes through lamp B. Calculate the energy transferred by lamp B.

c. Calculate the total energy transferred by both lamps during this period.

d. A total of 8 C of charge leaves the cell during this period. Using your answer to c, show that the potential difference across the cell must also be 4 V.

Resistance

potential difference (V) = current (A) x resistance (Ω)

1. Complete the following paragraph using the words below.

resistance   ohm   electrons   thermal   coulomb   component

An electrical current is a flow of _____ around a circuit. These carry energy. When the

electrons pass through a _____ they collide with atoms in the metal. The energy is

transferred to _____ energy. The _____ tells us the potential difference

required to drive one _____ of charge through. The unit for resistance is the _____ (Ω).

2. The circuit on the right has a current of 0.2 A. The potential difference across the lamp is 10 V.

Calculate the resistance of the lamp.

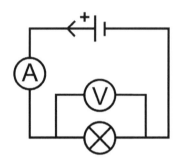

Resistance of lamp = _____ Ω

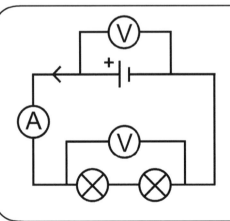

3. The circuit on the left has a current of 0.3 A. The combined resistance of the lamps is 20 Ω .

Calculate the total potential difference across the lamps.

Potential difference = _____ V

4. The circuit on the right has a potential difference of 5 V across the cell. The lamp has a resistance of 50 Ω.

Calculate the current flowing through the circuit.

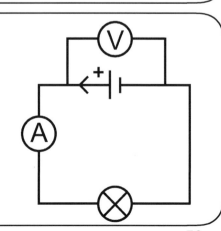

Current = _____ A

Resistors

1. The circuit on the right shows a resistor in series with a lamp.

a. Using the idea of energy transfer, explain how using the resistor reduces the brightness of the lamp.

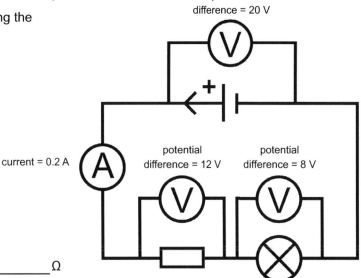

potential difference = 20 V

potential difference = 12 V   potential difference = 8 V

current = 0.2 A

b. Calculate the resistance of the resistor.

Resistance of resistor = _____ Ω

c. Calculate the resistance of the lamp.

Resistance of lamp = _____ Ω

2. If we increase the potential difference across a resistor and measure the current, we get the graph on the right.

a. Explain how the shape of the graph tells us that the current is directly proportional to the potential difference.

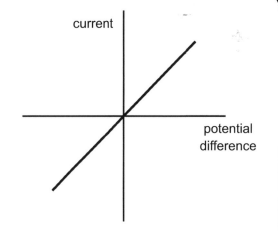

current

potential difference

b. Select the correct words from the boxes to complete the sentences below.

Because a resistor gives us a straight line graph, this tells us that the
| current |
| resistance |
| potential difference |
is constant.

This kind of resistor is called an
| open |
| organic |
| ohmic |
conductor. This is only the case if the temperature is
| constant |
| high |
| low |
.

Resistance of a Filament Lamp

1. We often use filament lamps in electrical circuits in schools.

a. What is meant by the word "filament"?

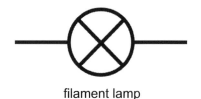

filament lamp

b. Explain why a filament glows when a current is running through it.

2. If we increase the potential difference across a filament lamp and measure the current, we get the graph on the right.

Explain how the shape of the graph tells us that the current through a filament lamp is not directly proportional to the potential difference.

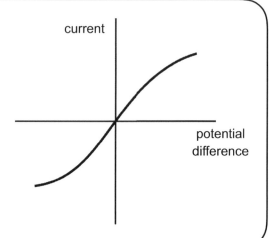

current

potential difference

3. The diagrams below show the atoms in a filament under cool conditions and under hot conditions. Delocalised electrons are shown in black.

a. Using the diagrams, explain why the resistance of the filament increases as it gets hot.

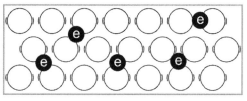

Cool conditions

b. Explain why a filament lamp is not an ohmic conductor.

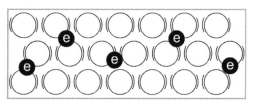

Hot conditions

Diodes and LEDs

1. Circuits often contain a diode.

a. Which of the following is the correct symbol for a diode?

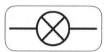  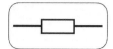

b. The two circuits below both contain a diode. In which of the two circuits will the lamp light up? Explain your answer.

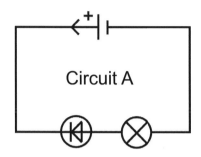 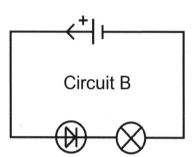

Explanation:

c. Sketch the shape of the current-potential difference graph for a diode on the axes below.

current

potential
difference

Exam tip: A very common question is to ask you to select the correct current-potential difference graph for an ohmic conductor, a filament lamp and a diode. So it's really important that you learn them.

2. The symbol for a light-emitting diode (LED) is shown on the right.

a. Describe one similarity and one difference between a light-emitting diode and a normal diode.

light-emitting diode

Similarity

Difference

b. Describe one advantage of using an LED in a circuit rather than a filament lamp.

Resistors in Series and Parallel

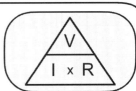

1. The diagram shows a circuit containing two resistors in series.

a. Determine the combined resistance of the two resistors.

b. Calculate the current flowing around the circuit.

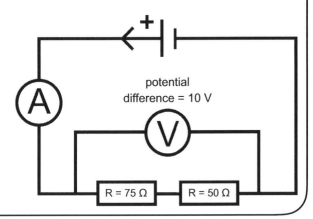

potential difference = 10 V

R = 75 Ω   R = 50 Ω

---

2. The diagram shows a circuit containing three resistors in series.

a. Use the current and potential difference to calculate the total resistance of the circuit.

b. Calculate the resistance of the first resistor.

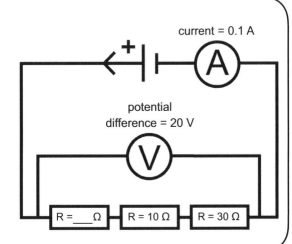

current = 0.1 A

potential difference = 20 V

R = ___ Ω   R = 10 Ω   R = 30 Ω

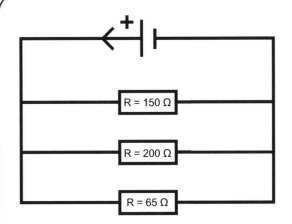

R = 150 Ω

R = 200 Ω

R = 65 Ω

b. Explain your answer to part a.

3. The circuit on the left contains resistors in parallel.

a. Select the value for the total resistance of the circuit.

Greater than 200 Ω

Between 150 Ω - 200 Ω

Less than 65 Ω

Light-Dependent Resistors

1. Light-dependent resistors (LDRs) are often found in circuits. The symbol for an LDR is shown on the right.

The resistance of an LDR varies with light intensity. This is shown on the graph.

Describe how the resistance of an LDR varies with light intensity.

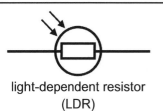

light-dependent resistor
(LDR)

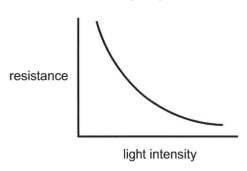

resistance

light intensity

2. Light-dependent resistors are used to turn circuits on or off depending on the light intensity.

A good example is a mobile phone screen turning off when the phone is placed to your ear.

The diagram below shows a circuit with an LDR in light conditions.

a. Calculate the total resistance of the circuit under light conditions.

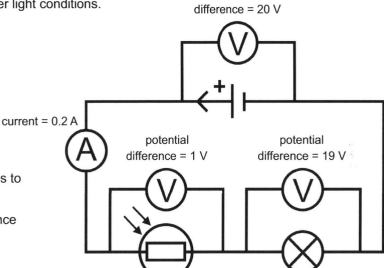

potential difference = 20 V

current = 0.2 A

potential difference = 1 V

potential difference = 19 V

lamp = on

b. In the dark, the resistance of the LDR increases to 10 000 Ω.

Describe the effect of this on the potential difference across the LDR.

c. In the dark, the total resistance of the circuit increases to over 10 000 Ω.

Describe the effect of this on the current running through the circuit.

d. State what happens to the lamp in dark conditions.

Thermistors

1. The symbols below show three different types of resistors.

a. Draw lines to connect each type of resistor to the correct symbol.

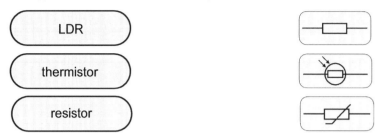

b. Draw a line on the axes to show how the resistance of a thermistor depends on the temperature.

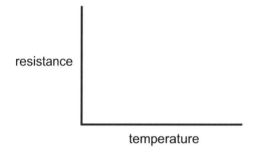

c. Thermistors are often found in thermostats. What is meant by a thermostat?

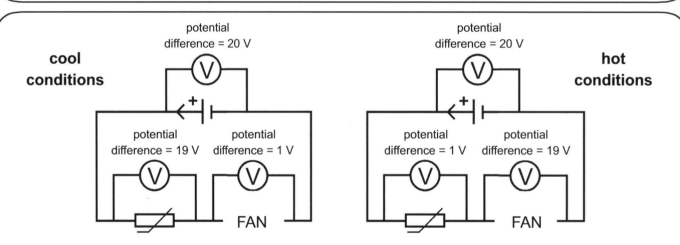

cool conditions   **hot conditions**

2. The diagrams above show a thermistor used to control a cooling fan in a computer.

a. Use the diagrams to explain why the fan turns on in hot conditions.

b. Explain how a thermistor is used in incubators for premature babies.

Required Practical: Resistance

1. In this practical, we are going to measure how the resistance of a wire changes as we increase the length of the wire.

The diagrams below show the circuit that we use for this practical. Complete the diagrams to show the labels of the important components.

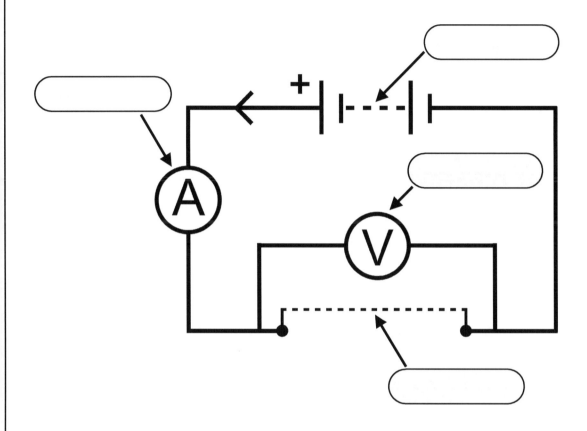

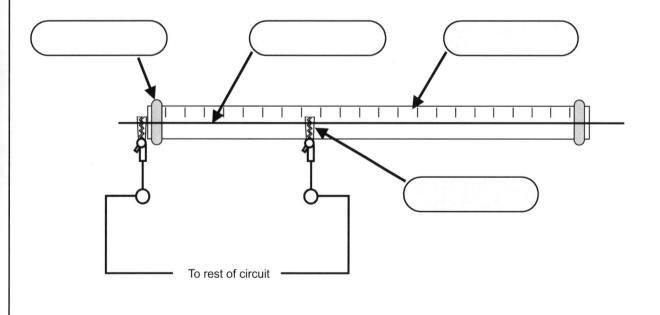

To rest of circuit

2. The stages below show how to carry out the practical. Use the words from the box to complete the stages.

1. Adjust the _____ to the zero position on the metre ruler.

2. Use the _____ to measure the current running through the circuit.

3. Use the voltmeter to measure the _____ across the wire.

4. Calculate the _____ of the wire.

5. Now adjust the crocodile clip to change the _____ of the wire and calculate the resistance for each length.

> resistance
> crocodile clip
> ammeter
> length
> potential difference

---

3. The graph below shows how the resistance of the wire depends on the length of the wire.

a. Explain how the graph shows that the resistance of the wire is directly proportional to the length of the wire.

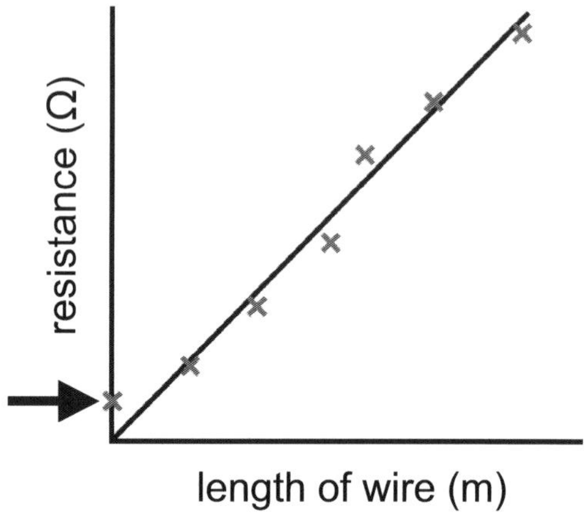

b. The point labelled on the graph is a zero error.

Explain what is meant by a zero error.

c. A zero error is a problem due to the equipment. It cannot be reduced by doing repeats.

What do scientists call errors like zero error?

(Random error)   (Human error)   (Systematic error)

d. How should we deal with a zero error such as the one in this practical?

e. State two causes of the zero error in this experiment.

4. One of the problems with this practical is that the temperature of the wire can increase.

a. Explain why the wire getting warm will be a problem.

b. One way of addressing this problem is to use a low potential difference.
Explain how this will help to reduce the problem.

c. Suggest another way that we can reduce the problem of heating in the wire.

5. The circuit below contains a variable resistor. Variable resistors contain a long piece of wire.

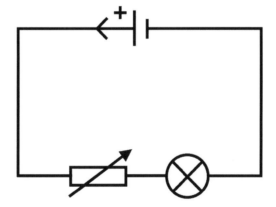

Select the correct words from the boxes to complete the sentences below.

A variable resistor allows us to change the resistance by changing the

| thickness |
| length |
| temperature |

of the wire.

If we increase the

| current |
| resistance |
| potential difference |

then the lamp will

| become brighter. |
| stay the same. |
| become dimmer. |

1. In this practical, we are going to investigate how the current running through a component changes with the potential difference across the component.

We start by investigating a fixed resistor. The diagram below shows the circuit that we use for this practical.

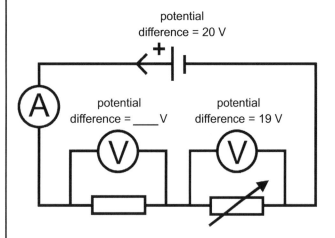

potential
difference = 20 V

potential
difference = ____ V

potential
difference = 19 V

A

a. Label the variable resistor in the circuit.

b. First we adjust the variable resistor so that it has a high resistance. This means that the potential difference across the variable resistor is high.

Complete the diagram to show the potential difference across the fixed resistor.

Next we read the current on the ammeter.

We now adjust the variable resistor.

By changing the potential difference across the variable resistor, we can change the potential difference across the fixed resistor.

We get a graph like the one shown on the right.

This shows that the current through a fixed resistor is **directly proportional** to the potential difference across the resistor.

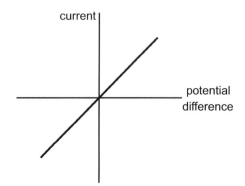

current

potential difference

c. Explain how the graph shows that the current is directly proportional to the potential difference.

d. What name do scientists give to conductors which show a current-potential difference graph like this?

e. Why is it important not to leave the above circuit connected for too long?

2. We now repeat the experiment but this time using a filament lamp. The circuit and current-potential difference graph are shown below.

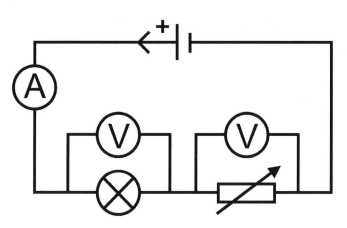
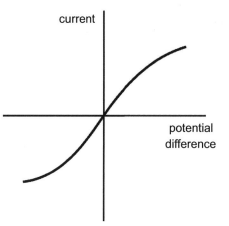

Which of the following are true about a filament lamp? Tick the correct boxes.

> The current through a filament lamp is directly proportional to the potential difference

> A filament lamp is not an ohmic conductor

> The resistance of a filament lamp is constant

> At a high potential difference, the resistance of the filament lamp increases as it gets hotter

3. The experiment is now repeated using a diode. The circuit and current-potential difference graph for a diode is shown below.

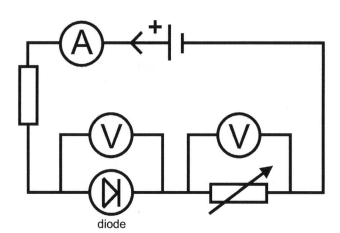
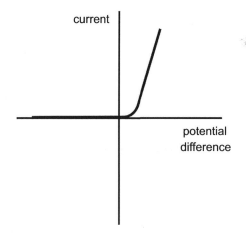

diode

a. Describe how the current changes with potential difference for a diode.

b. Explain why no current flows through a diode if the potential difference is reversed.

Energy Transfer by Appliances

1. Electrical appliances transfer energy from one energy store to another.

a. Draw a line to connect each appliance to the intended energy transfer.

| Washing machine | Iron | Kettle |

| Energy transferred to thermal energy store | Energy transferred to kinetic energy store |

| Blender | Hairdryer | Fan |

b. In both a fan and a blender, a small amount of the energy is transferred to the thermal energy store.

Explain why we do not consider this when looking at the energy transfer in these appliances.

c. State the intended energy transfers taking place in the following electrical appliances.

Hair straighteners _____   Microwave oven _____

Exam tip: Remember that you only need to consider appliances which transfer energy to the kinetic energy store, the thermal energy store or both.

2. The energy transfer carried out by an appliance is given by its power rating.

The power ratings of a fan and a clothes dryer are shown below.

| Fan
Power rating = 25 W | Clothes Dryer
Power rating = 1000 W |

a. The unit for power is the watt (W).

Complete the sentence below.

1 watt is 1_____ of energy transferred by an appliance every_____

b. Explain why the clothes dryer has a much greater power rating than a fan.

Calculating Energy Transferred by Appliances

Exam tip: You are not given this equation in the exam.

energy transferred (J) = power (W) x time (s)

E / P x t

1. Calculate the total energy transferred by the following appliances.

a. A set of hair straighteners has a power of 170 W.

These are used for 140 seconds.

Total energy transferred = _____ J

b. An electric toothbrush has a power of 2 W.

It is used for 2 minutes.

Total energy transferred = _____ J

c. A lamp has a power of 7 W.

It is used for three hours.

Total energy transferred = _____ J

d. A television has a power of 100 W.

It is used for five hours.

Total energy transferred = _____ kJ

2. Calculate the power rating of the following appliances.

a. An electric shaver is used for 300 seconds.

A total of 900 J of energy is transferred.

Power rating = _____ W

b. A toaster is used for two minutes.

A total of 240 kJ of energy is transferred.

Power rating = _____ W

c. A vacuum cleaner is used for twenty minutes.

A total of 144 kJ of energy is transferred.

Power rating = _____ W

3. Calculate the time that the following appliances were used for.

a. A microwave oven has a power rating of 900 W. A total of 432 kJ of energy was transferred.

Time = _____ s

b. A washing machine has a power rating of 500 W. A total of 900 kJ of energy was transferred.

Time = _____ s

Power of Components

power (W) = potential difference (V) x current (A)

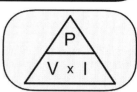

1. Calculate the power of the resistor in the circuit on the left.

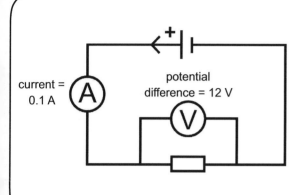

current = 0.1 A

potential difference = 12 V

2. Calculate the power of resistor B in the circuit on the left.

To answer this question you will first need to work out the potential difference across resistor B.

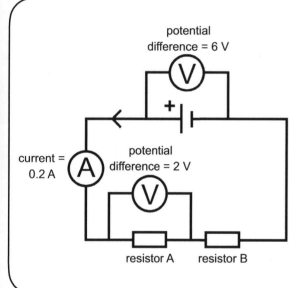

potential difference = 6 V

current = 0.2 A

potential difference = 2 V

resistor A   resistor B

3. Calculate the power of resistor A in the circuit on the right.

To answer this question you will first need to work out the potential difference across resistor A.

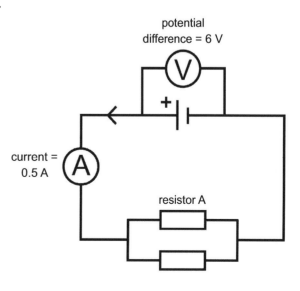

potential difference = 6 V

current = 0.5 A

resistor A

4. Calculate the current in the circuit on the right.

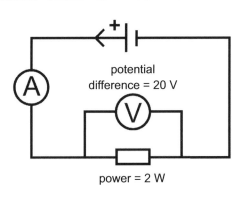

potential
difference = 20 V

power = 2 W

---

5. Calculate the current in the top branch of the circuit on the left.

potential
difference = 15 V

power = 3 W

---

6. Calculate the potential difference across the resistor in the
circuit on the right.

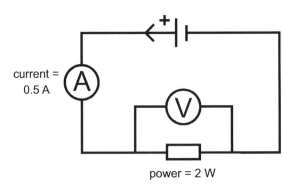

current =
0.5 A

power = 2 W

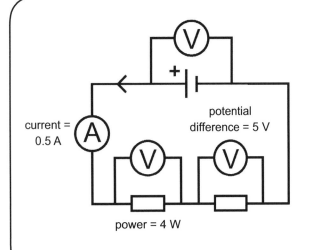

current =
0.5 A

potential
difference = 5 V

power = 4 W

7. The circuit on the left shows two resistors in series.

a. Calculate the potential difference across the resistor on the
left.

b. From your answer to part a, determine the potential
difference across the cell.

power (W) = current^2 (A) x resistance (Ω)

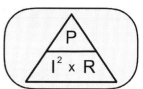

8. The circuit on the right shows two resistors in series.

Calculate the power of resistor B.

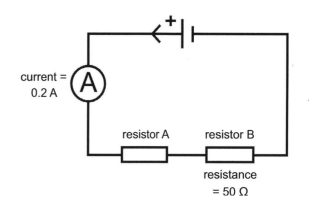

current = 0.2 A

resistor A   resistor B

resistance = 50 Ω

9. Calculate the resistance of the lamp in the circuit on the left.

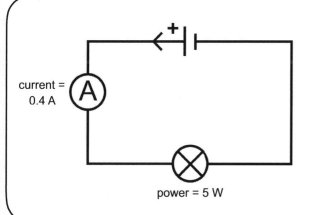

current = 0.4 A

power = 5 W

10. The circuit below shows three resistors in series.

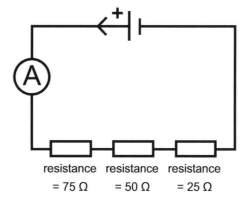

resistance = 75 Ω   resistance = 50 Ω   resistance = 25 Ω

a. Calculate the total resistance of the three resistors.

b. The total power of the circuit is 24 W. Calculate the current in the circuit.

DC and AC Supply

1. Complete the following paragraph using the words below.

230 V   transformer   switches   direct   rises   one   50 Hz   alternating   potential difference

The electrical supply from a cell is an example of _____ current. This is because the current

moves in _____ direction only and the _____ does not change. Mains

electricity is an _____ current. With AC, the current _____ direction many

times every second and the potential difference _____ and falls. The benefit of AC is that

we can use a _____ to easily change the potential difference of the supply. Mains

electricity has a frequency of _____ and a potential difference of around _____ .

2. The oscilloscope traces show two different electrical supplies (not from the UK).

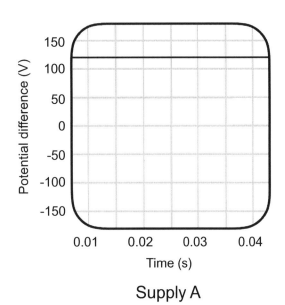

Supply A

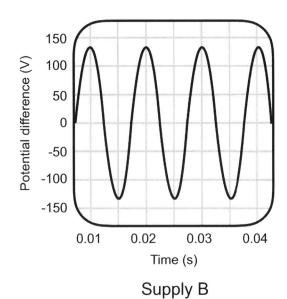

Supply B

a. Explain how the trace shows that supply A is a direct current supply.

b. Calculate the frequency of the alternating current of supply B.

Mains Electricity

1. In the UK, electrical appliances are connected to the power supply using a three-core cable. This is shown in the diagram below.

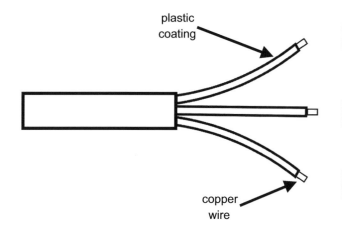

plastic coating

copper wire

Brown wire = _____

Blue wire = _____

Green / Yellow striped wire = _____

a. Explain why the wires are made of copper.

b. Why are the coatings made of plastic?

c. Complete the boxes to show the live wire, the neutral wire and the earth wire.

2. Draw lines to connect the correct cable to the correct function.

Live wire

Neutral wire

Earth wire

This wire normally has a potential difference of 0 V. If there is a fault so the casing of the appliance becomes live, this wire carries the current to Earth. This causes the fuse to melt, shutting off the current.

This wire carries the electrical current from the generators and always has a potential difference of around 230 V. This wire can be dangerous even if a switch in the mains circuit is open.

The job of this wire is to complete the circuit.

3. The diagram below shows the electrical supply to an appliance such as a washing machine.

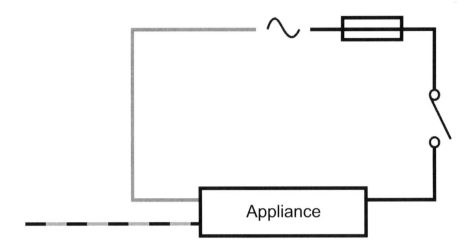

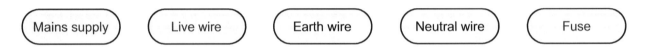

a. Label the diagram using the labels below.

(Mains supply)   (Live wire)   (Earth wire)   (Neutral wire)   (Fuse)

b. Explain why the live wire can be dangerous even if the switch is open.

c. Explain why the neutral wire cannot carry a current if the switch is open.

d. Sometimes a fault can develop within an appliance so that the metal casing is connected to the live wire. If this happens, then the casing is now live. If a person touches the casing, electricity can flow through the person to Earth. The person is electrocuted and this could be fatal.

Explain how the Earth wire and the fuse act together to prevent electrocution.

The National Grid

1. The National Grid distributes electricity from power stations to homes, factories and offices.

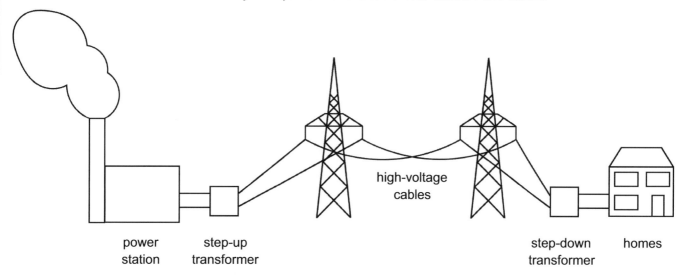

power
station

step-up
transformer

high-voltage
cables

step-down
transformer

homes

a. Circle the box below which correctly describes the National Grid.

| Power stations and high voltage cables | Power stations and transformers | Transformers and high-voltage cables |

b. The following paragraph contains a number of mistakes. Rewrite the paragraph correctly in the space below.

Electricity has to be transmitted from power stations to homes, offices and factories. The problem is that a lot of electricity is lost in the transmission cables. One way to reduce this is to build houses far away from power stations. However, this is not a realistic solution. Another way is to transmit the electricity at very low potential difference.

First the electricity passes through step-down transformers which increase the potential difference to several hundred thousand volts. The electricity then passes through high-voltage cables. Finally, step-up transformers decrease the potential difference to 230 volts before the electricity is passed to homes.

Static Electricity

1. Tick the correct box for each sentence and then write out any false statement correctly below.

	True	False
Materials such as plastic are good conductors of electricity	☐	☐
Conductors have electrons which can easily move through them	☐	☐
Insulators include metals	☐	☐
Insulators do not have electrons which can move through them	☐	☐

2. A student rubbed a plastic rod against a cloth.

The cloth became negatively charged and the rod became positively charged.

a. Explain in terms of electrons why these charges formed.

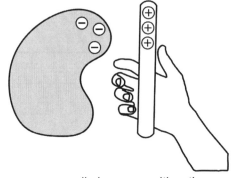

b. The student now rubbed the cloth against a metal rod. Afterwards, there was no overall charge on either the cloth or the metal rod.

Explain why not.

3. During refuelling, jet fuel can become charged as it passes through the pipes. Explain why the refuelling truck and the airplane are both earthed.

Electric Fields

1. The diagrams below show plastic spheres with charges.

a. Draw arrows to show the forces between the spheres.

In each case, explain your answer and describe how the spheres would move.

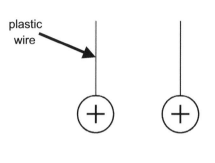

Explanation:

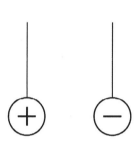

Explanation:

b. Describe what would happen if the spheres were held by copper wire rather than plastic wires.

Explain your answer.

2. Select the correct word from the boxes to complete the sentences below.

Two charges which are the same will

> have no effect on
> repel
> attract

each other. However, if the two charges are

different then they will

> have no effect on
> repel
> attract

each other. The forces which exist between charges are called

> contact
> non-contact
> external

forces as the two objects do not need to touch for the forces to operate.

3. When a person walked across a carpet, electrons moved from the carpet on to the person. This made the person negatively charged.

The person noticed that the hairs on their head stood up. Explain why this happened.

4. The diagram below shows four different field diagrams. Each one has a mistake.

Next to each diagram, describe the mistake and draw the correct version.

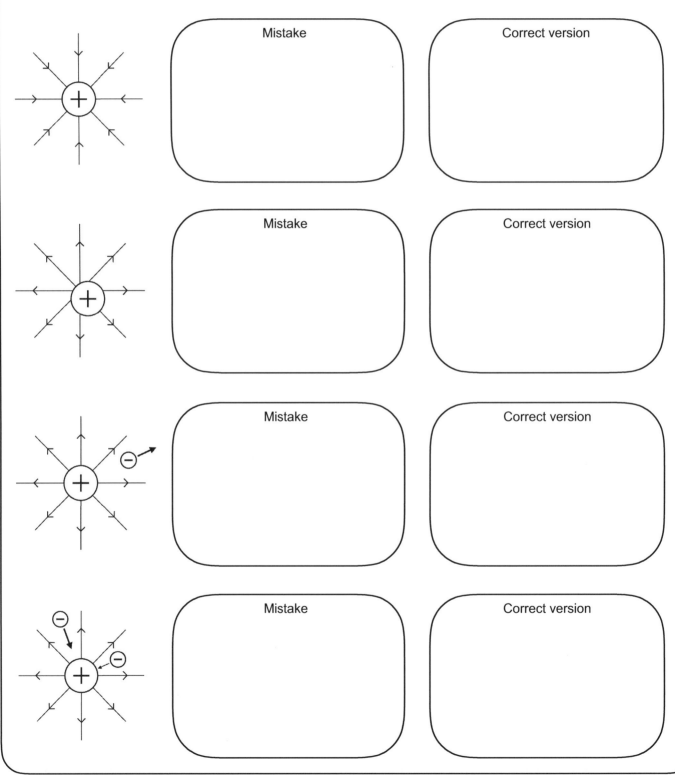

Mistake	Correct version
Mistake	Correct version
Mistake	Correct version
Mistake	Correct version

Chapter 3: Particle Model of Matter

- Describe the spacing, arrangement and movement of particles in solids, liquids and gases and use these to explain the density of solids, liquids and gases.

- Calculate the density of an object.

- Describe how to determine the density of a regular-shaped and an irregular-shaped object (required practical).

- Describe what is meant by internal energy.

- Explain why internal energy changes when a substance changes state.

- Explain why a change of state is a physical process but not a chemical process.

- Describe what happens to particles when a substance evaporates.

- Use the idea of specific heat capacity to make calculations involving the temperature change of substances.

- Interpret heating and cooling graphs to identify changes of state.

- Use the idea of internal energy to explain why changes of state do not involve a change in temperature.

- Use the idea of specific latent heat to make calculations involving changes of state.

- Describe how the movement of gas particles can be used to explain gas pressure.

- Explain why the pressure of a gas increases when the temperature increases.

- Carry out calculations involving gas pressure and gas volume.

- Explain how compressing a gas involves doing work and use this to explain why compressing a gas can increase the temperature of the gas.

Density

1. The diagram below shows the particles in solids, liquids and gases.

a. Describe how the particles are arranged in the space next to each diagram.

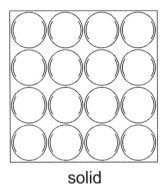

solid

Spacing of particles

Arrangement of particles

Movement of particles

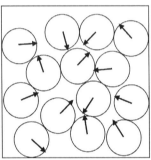

liquid

Spacing of particles

Arrangement of particles

Movement of particles

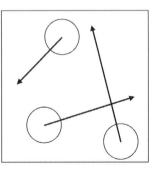

gas

Spacing of particles

Arrangement of particles

Movement of particles

b. Complete the following paragraph using the words below.

polystyrene   **mass**   **brick**   **density**

The_____ of a material tells us the_____ in a given volume.

A _____ is dense because it contains a lot of mass packed into its volume.

A _____ block is not dense as it only has a small mass in its volume.

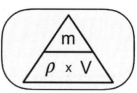

Exam tip: You are not given this equation in the exam.

density (kg/m³) $=$ $\dfrac{\text{mass (kg)}}{\text{volume (m}^3)}$

2. A sample of magnesium has a volume of 2 m³ and a mass of 3476 kg.

Calculate the density of magnesium.

Density = _____ kg / m³

3. A swimming pool has a volume of 600 m³. The water in the pool has a mass of 598 800 kg.

Calculate the density of the water.

Density = _____ kg / m³

4. A room has a volume of 72 m³. The air in the room has a mass of 88 kg.

Calculate the density of air. Give your answer to 2 significant figures.

Density = _____ kg / m³

5. The diagrams show the arrangement of particles in a solid, a liquid and a gas.

Use the diagrams to explain why the density of solids and liquids is much greater than the density of a gas.

solid

liquid

gas

6. Polystyrene is an example of a solid with a low density.

Explain why polystyrene has a low density. You should refer to the arrangement of particles in your answer.

Required Practical: Density

Exam tip: You have to be able to describe how to determine the density of objects with a regular shape and also objects with an irregular shape.

1. To determine the density of an object with a regular shape such as a cube or cuboid, we first measure its mass using a balance.

We then measure the length of the sides of the cube or cuboid in metres.

From this, we can work out the volume in m³. To calculate the volume, we multiply the lengths of all of the sides.

Finally, we use the equation for density to determine the density of the cube.

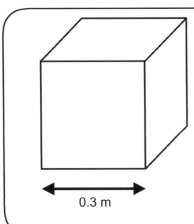

0.3 m

a. The mass of this cube is 27 kg.

Determine the density of the cube.

Density = _____ kg / m³

b. The mass of this cube is 12 kg.

Determine the density of the cube.

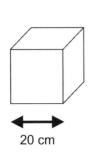

20 cm

Density = _____ kg / m³

c. The mass of this cuboid is 12 000 g.

Determine the density of the cuboid.

0.3 m

0.4 m

0.5 m

Density = _____ kg / m³

2. To determine the density of an object with an irregular shape, we use a displacement method.

a. Just like with a regular object we need to find the mass of the object using a balance.

What do we need to do with the mass before calculating the density?

300 g

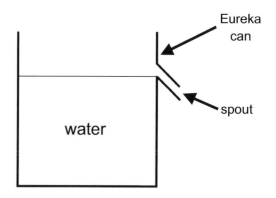

Eureka can

spout

water

b. We now fill a Eureka can with water so that the water overflows from the spout.

Suggest why it is important that the water overflows from the spout.

c. Next we place the object into the water.

Some of the water will overflow from the Eureka can.

We need to measure the volume of water displaced using a measuring cylinder.

Why is it important that we measure the volume of water using a measuring cylinder rather than a beaker?

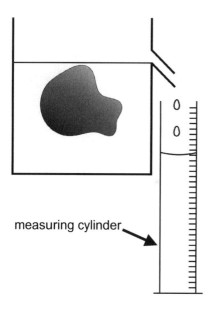

measuring cylinder

d. The irregular object had a mass of 2 kg and a volume of 0.0004 m³.

Calculate the density of the irregular object.

Density = _____ kg / m³

Internal Energy

1. Select the correct words from the boxes to complete the sentences below.

When particles are moving, they have [thermal / **kinetic** / sound] energy. Gases have the most and solids have the least.

Particles also have [forces / charges / links] between them. There are also [links / charges / bonds] between the atoms in a molecule.

The energy in forces and bonds is called [thermal / potential / elastic] energy. The kinetic energy of the particles added to

the potential energy of the forces and bonds is called the [total / overall / internal] energy.

2. The changes of state between solids, liquids and gases are shown below.

a. Label the changes of state using the words below.

boiling   **freezing**   **condensation**   **melting**   **sublimation**

b. Write a plus sign next to changes of state where internal energy increases and a minus sign where it decreases.

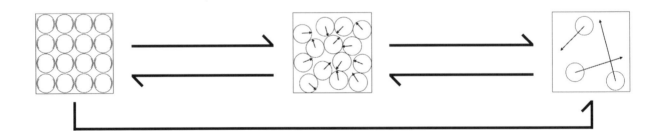

c. Explain why change of state does not involve a change in mass.

d. Change of state is a physical not a chemical process. What does this mean?

e. Explain in terms of particles what happens during evaporation.

Specific Heat Capacity

change in thermal energy (J) = mass (kg) x specific heat capacity (J/kg °C) x temperature change (°C)

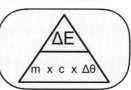

1. A radiator contains 30 kg of water. When the heating comes on, the temperature of the water increases from 20°C to 60°C.

Calculate the energy required to heat the water in the radiator. The specific heat capacity of water is 4200 J / kg °C.

Energy required = _____ kJ

2. A saucepan containing 2 kg of water is heated. 400 kJ of energy is transferred. Calculate the temperature increase of the water.

The specific heat capacity of water is 4200 J / kg °C. Give your answer to four significant figures.

Temperature increase = _____ °C

3. 900 kJ of energy was transferred into a block of steel. The temperature increased from 20°C to 50°C. Calculate the mass of the block.

The specific heat capacity of steel is 511 J / kg °C. Give your answer to three significant figures.

Mass of block = _____ kg

4. A copper block with a mass of 3 kg is heated from 20°C to 65°C. A total of 52 kJ of energy is transferred.

Calculate the specific heat capacity of copper. Give your answer to three significant figures.

Specific heat capacity of copper = _____ J / kg °C

Heating and Cooling Graphs

1. A student took a solid chemical and gently heated it. The heating graph is shown below.

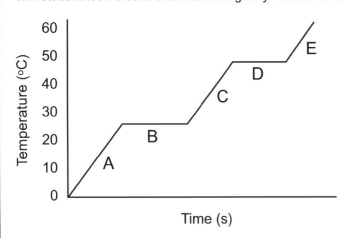

a. Explain why the temperature is rising at point A on the graph.

b. Label the graph to show the points when the substance is melting and boiling.

c. Using the graph, determine the approximate melting and boiling points of the chemical.

melting point =_____ °C

boiling point =_____ °C

d. Explain why the temperature stops rising when the chemical changes state, even though we are still putting energy in.

e. What do scientists call the energy required to change the state of a substance?

kinetic heat

specific heat

latent heat

f. Which points on the graph show the internal energy store increasing without breaking the forces of attraction between particles?

A only

B only

A + B

A, C and E

2. The diagram below shows a cooling graph for a different chemical.

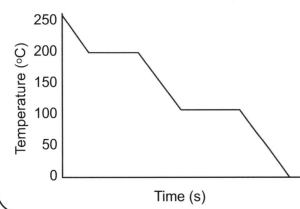

a. Label the graph to show where condensation and freezing take place.

b. Use the graph to determine the approximate condensation and freezing points of this chemical.

condensation point = ____ °C

freezing point = ____ °C

Specific Latent Heat

energy for a change of state (J) = mass (kg) x specific latent heat (J/kg)

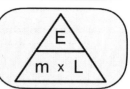

1. Complete the following paragraph using the words below.

melted   **boils**   **kilogram**   **fusion**   **temperature**   **vaporisation**

The specific latent heat of _____ is the energy required to change one _____

of a substance from a solid to a liquid with no change in _____ . This applies when a

substance is _____ . The specific latent heat of _____ is the energy required

to change one kilogram of a substance from a liquid to a vapour with no change in temperature. This

applies when a substance _____ .

2. Using the above equation, calculate the energy required for the following changes of state.

a. Calculate the energy required to melt 2 kg of candle wax.

The specific latent heat of fusion of candle wax is 200 000 J / kg.

Energy = _____ J

b. Calculate the energy required to boil 600 g of octane.

The specific latent heat of vaporisation of octane is 298 000 J / kg.

Energy = _____ J

c. 6.68 kJ of energy is required to melt the ice cubes in a drink.

Calculate the mass of the ice cubes. The specific latent leat of fusion of water is 334 000 J / kg.

Mass = _____ kg

Particle Motion in Gases

1. The diagrams below show two containers filled with an identical gas.

Both containers are at the same temperature and have the same volume.

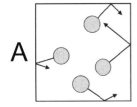 A

B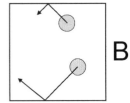

a. A student makes the following statement.

The pressure in the two containers will be the same as they are filled with an identical gas.

Explain why this student's statement is **not** correct.

b. Which of the following statements are correct?

| Container B will have a greater pressure than container A | Container A will have a greater pressure than container B | The pressure of container B will be half the pressure of container A |

c. Explain your answer to question b.

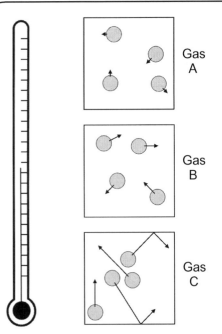

Gas A

Gas B

Gas C

2. The diagrams show three containers filled with an identical gas.

The containers are not at the same temperature.

The size of the arrows represents the **kinetic energy** of the particles.

a. Draw a line from each container to the correct point on the thermometer.

Explain your answer.

b. Which gas will be at the greatest pressure?

Explain your answer.

Pressure in Gases

1. When gas particles collide with the walls of a container, they create a force at right angles to the walls.

This force causes the pressure of the gas.

The two containers below have the same type of gas at the same temperature.

The volume of gas B is twice the volume of gas A.

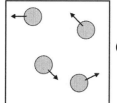 Gas A

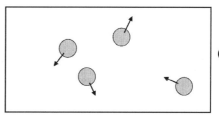 Gas B

Using the idea of collisions, explain why the pressure of gas A will be twice the pressure of gas B.

2. You need to be able to apply the equation above to changes in the pressure or volume of a gas.

a. A gas has a volume of 20 m³ and a pressure of 100 000 Pa. The volume is decreased to 10 m³.

Calculate the pressure of the gas.

b. A gas has a volume of 100 m³ and a pressure of 200 000 Pa. The volume of the gas is increased so that the pressure falls to 50 000 Pa.

Calculate the volume of the gas.

c. Explain how these questions show that the pressure of a gas is inversely proportional to its volume.

d. Why is it important that the temperature is kept constant when investigating how the pressure of a gas is affected by its volume?

Work Done on a Gas

Exam tip: Remember that work is when we use a force to transfer energy.
We'll see work again in Physics 2.

1. The diagram below shows a piston containing a gas, for example the type found in a bicycle pump.

The diagram shows before and after a force is used to compress the gas.

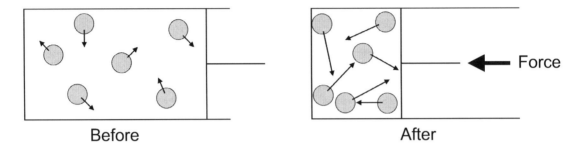

Before   After

a. Looking at the diagram, what has happened to the kinetic energy of the gas particles when a gas is compressed?

> The kinetic energy of the particles is unchanged

> The kinetic energy of the particles is increased

> The kinetic energy of the particles is reduced

b. Explain how compressing a gas is an example of work.

c. When we carry out work on a gas, we transfer energy to the internal energy store of the gas particles. State the two energy stores that make up internal energy.

d. Select the correct words from the boxes to complete the sentences below.

When we compress a gas, we increase the [elastic / internal / electrical] energy of the particles. Because the particles now have

a greater kinetic energy, the [volume / latent heat / temperature] of the gas increases.

This explains why the end of a bicycle pump [heats up / cools down / stays constant] when we inflate a tyre.

Chapter 4: Atomic Structure and Radioactivity

• State the radius of a typical atom and the radius of the nucleus.
• Label a diagram of the structure of an atom.
• State the charges on protons, neutrons and electrons.
• Describe how electromagnetic radiation can be absorbed or emitted when electrons change energy levels.
• Use the atomic number and mass number to determine the number of protons, neutrons and electrons in atoms of an element.
• Describe what is meant by an isotope.
• Describe what is meant by an ion and explain how atoms can form positive ions.
• Describe the features of the plum-pudding model of atomic structure.
• Describe the results of the alpha-scattering experiment and explain how these results were used to determine the nuclear model of atomic structure.
• Describe how the scientists Niels Bohr and James Chadwick further developed the nuclear model of atomic structure.
• Describe what is meant by radioactivity and how radioactivity is a random process.
• Describe what is meant by alpha, beta and gamma radiation and their properties.
• Write nuclear equations for radioactive decay.
• Calculate the half-life for a radioactive isotope and determine the number of undecayed nuclei after a given number of half-lives.
• Describe the differences between irradiation and contamination and how irradiation / contamination can be prevented or reduced.
• Describe what is meant by background radiation and the sources of this.
• Describe how nuclear radiation can be used in medicine.
• Explain what is meant by nuclear fission and a chain reaction.
• Describe what is meant by nuclear fusion.

Atomic Structure

1. The diagram below shows the structure of an atom (not to scale).

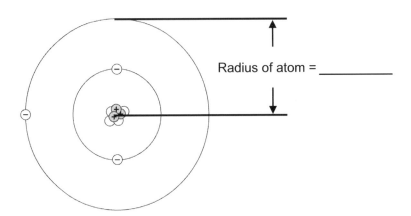

Radius of atom = _____

a. Which of the following shows the typical radius of an atom?

1×10^{-8} m 1×10^{-9} m 1×10^{-10} m

b. Label the diagram to show the radius of the atom.

c. The radius of the nucleus is less than 1 / 10 000th the radius of the atom.

Which of the following shows the radius of the nucleus?

less than 1×10^{-12} m   less than 1×10^{-13} m   less than 1×10^{-14} m

d. On the diagram below, draw an arrow from each label to the correct part of the atom.

proton   nucleus

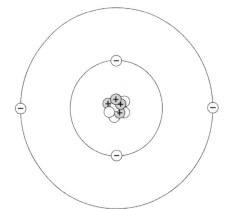

neutron   electron

e. Protons, neutrons and electrons are called subatomic particles. Draw a line to link the correct subatomic particle with the correct charge.

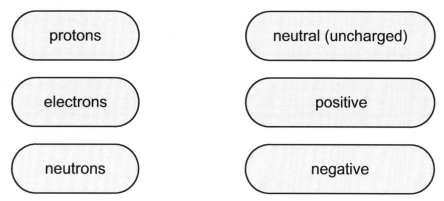

protons   neutral (uncharged)

electrons   positive

neutrons   negative

f. Explain why the nucleus has an overall positive charge.

g. Why does the charge on the nucleus not depend on the number of neutrons?

h. The diagram below shows two atoms which are absorbing or emitting electromagnetic radiation.

In each case, state whether electromagnetic radiation is being absorbed or emitted and explain your answer.

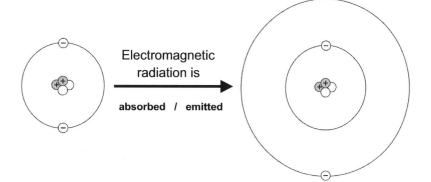

Electromagnetic radiation is

absorbed / emitted

Explanation:

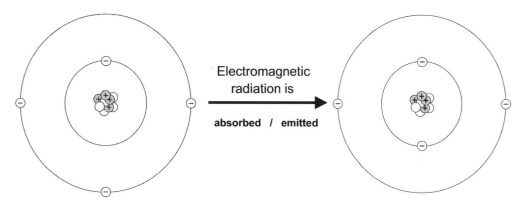

Electromagnetic radiation is

absorbed / emitted

Explanation:

i. On the two diagrams above, label the energy levels which are at the highest energy.

Atomic and Mass Numbers

Exam tip: Many students make mistakes when calculating the number of neutrons. You need to be certain that you can do this correctly each time.

1. The diagram on the right shows the symbol for the element potassium.

a. Label the atomic number on the diagram.

b. State the number of protons and electrons in atoms of potassium.

$$^{39}_{19}K$$

(protons_____)   (electrons_____)

c. Explain why atoms have no overall charge.

2. The diagram on the right shows the symbol for the element aluminium.

a. Label the mass number on the diagram.

b. Describe how to use the atomic number and mass number to calculate the number of neutrons in an atom of an element.

$$^{27}_{13}Al$$

c. State the number of protons, neutrons and electrons in the following elements.

$$^{11}_{5}B$$

protons = _____
neutrons = _____
electrons = _____

$$^{31}_{15}P$$

protons = _____
neutrons = _____
electrons = _____

$$^{40}_{18}Ar$$

protons = _____
neutrons = _____
electrons = _____

$$^{56}_{26}Fe$$

protons = _____
neutrons = _____
electrons = _____

$$^{80}_{35}Br$$

protons = _____
neutrons = _____
electrons = _____

$$^{88}_{38}Sr$$

protons = _____
neutrons = _____
electrons = _____

3. Three isotopes of carbon are shown below.

$^{12}_{6}C$

protons = _____

neutrons = _____

electrons = _____

$^{13}_{6}C$

protons = _____

neutrons = _____

electrons = _____

$^{14}_{6}C$

protons = _____

neutrons = _____

electrons = _____

a. Determine the numbers of protons, neutrons and electrons in these three isotopes.

b. Explain how these are all isotopes of carbon.

4. Atoms can form ions by losing electrons.

a. Describe what is meant by the word "ion".

b. Explain why an atom becomes a positive ion after losing an electron.

c. Determine the number of protons, neutrons and electrons in the following ions.

$^{7}_{3}Li^{+}$

protons = _____

neutrons = _____

electrons = _____

$^{24}_{12}Mg^{2+}$

protons = _____

neutrons = _____

electrons = _____

d. Question 2c shows six different elements. Two of these elements are described below.

In each case, determine the identity of the element. Explain your answer.

• This element can form a positive ion with a charge of +2. The ion has a total of 24 electrons.

Element =

Explanation:

• This element forms a positive ion with a charge of +3. The ion has a total of 2 electrons.

Element =

Explanation:

Alpha-Scattering and the Nuclear Model

Exam tip: Scientific models change as new evidence is produced.
The alpha-scattering experiment is a great example of this and is a favourite with examiners.

1. The idea of atoms has been around for a long time.

a. Complete the following paragraph using the words below.

electrons   **divided**   **internal**   **negative**

The ancient Greeks believed that atoms are tiny spheres that could not be_____ .

Centuries later, scientists found that atoms contain tiny_____ particles which they called

_____ . This showed scientists that atoms are not tiny spheres. Atoms must have an

_____ structure.

b. The first model of atomic structure was called the **plum-pudding model**.

A diagram of the plum-pudding model is shown on the right.

State the two key features of the plum-pudding model.

plum-pudding model

2. In order to see if the plum-pudding model was correct, scientists carried out the alpha-scattering experiment.

Alpha particles are tiny, positively charged particles which travel extremely quickly.

a. What did the scientists do in the alpha-scattering experiment?

b. Explain why the scientists used gold foil rather than any other type of metal.

3. The diagrams below show the results of the alpha-scattering experiment.

a. For each result, describe what the scientists found and then explain what this told the scientists about the structure of atoms.

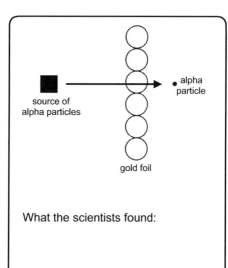

What the scientists found:

What this told the scientists:

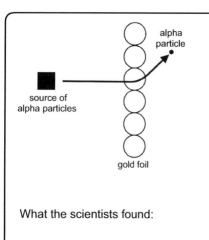

What the scientists found:

What this told the scientists:

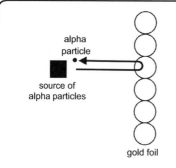

What the scientists found:

What this told the scientists:

b. From the results of the alpha-scattering experiment, scientists realised that the plum-pudding model was wrong. Scientists then developed the nuclear model of atomic structure.

Over time, the nuclear model also changed.

Link the correct statement to the correct version of the nuclear model below.

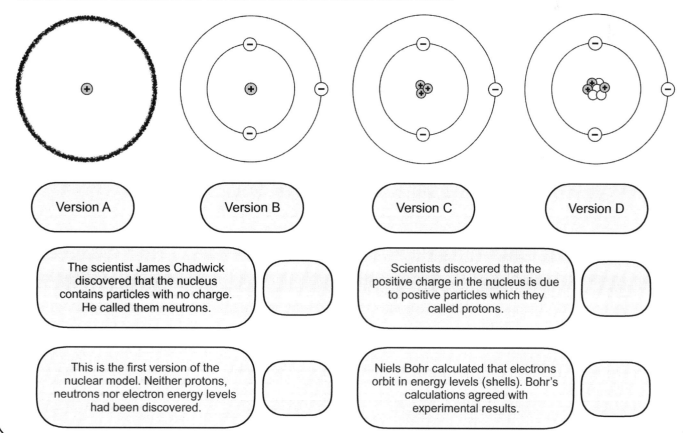

Version A

Version B

Version C

Version D

The scientist James Chadwick discovered that the nucleus contains particles with no charge. He called them neutrons.

Scientists discovered that the positive charge in the nucleus is due to positive particles which they called protons.

This is the first version of the nuclear model. Neither protons, neutrons nor electron energy levels had been discovered.

Niels Bohr calculated that electrons orbit in energy levels (shells). Bohr's calculations agreed with experimental results.

Radioactivity

1. Two isotopes of the element potassium are shown below.

$^{39}_{19}$K

protons_____   neutrons_____

electrons_____

$^{40}_{19}$K

protons_____   neutrons_____

electrons_____

a. Determine the number of protons, neutrons and electrons in these two isotopes.

b. Using your answer to **a**, explain how we know that these are isotopes.

c. Potassium-40 is a radioactive isotope. What is meant by "radioactive"? Use the words "unstable" and "radiation" in your answer.

d. Radioactive decay is a random process. Circle the correct box to show what this means.

| Scientists cannot predict whether an isotope will be radioactive | Scientists cannot predict which type of radiation will be emitted by a nucleus | Scientists cannot predict when any individual nucleus will decay |

e. A radioactive isotope has an activity of 50 Bq. How many nuclei will have decayed after three minutes?

f. A scientist used a Geiger-Muller tube to measure the count rate of a radioactive sample. Explain why the count rate will not be the same as the activity.

2. There are four different types of radiation that can be emitted from radioactive isotopes.

Draw a line to link the correct type of radiation to the correct description and the correct picture.

Alpha (α)

This is a type of electromagnetic radiation from the nucleus.

Beta (β)

This is sometimes given out by an unstable nucleus.

Gamma (γ)

This consists of two protons and two neutrons (the same as a helium nucleus).

neutron

A neutron changes to a proton and an electron. The electron is ejected from the nucleus.

Properties of Alpha, Beta and Gamma Radiation

Exam tip: The ranges in air and penetrating power of radiation are approximate and often cover a range of values. The values below are worth learning though.

1. The ranges in air of alpha, beta and gamma radiation are shown below (not to scale).

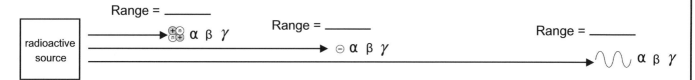

a. Circle the correct type of radiation above.

b. Complete the diagram by writing in the approximate range in air for each type of radiation.

c. Explain why alpha particles stop after travelling a short distance in air.

d. Which of the following could explain why beta particles travel further in air than alpha particles? Tick one box.

Beta particles have a positive charge	◯
Beta particles are smaller than alpha particles	◯
Beta particles are larger than alpha particles	◯

2. We can also measure the penetrating power of each type of radiation.

a. What is meant by penetrating power?

b. Complete the table to show how each type of radiation can be stopped. Use the selection on the right.

Type of radiation	Penetrating power
Alpha (α)	
Beta (β)	
Gamma (γ)	

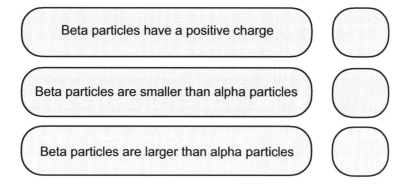

Stopped by several cm of lead

Stopped by a few mm of aluminium

Stopped by a single sheet of paper

3. The three different types of radiation have different ionising powers. This tells us how likely they are to form ions.

a. Explain how radiation can cause the formation of ions.

b. Rank the different types of radiation by the amount of ionisation that they can cause.

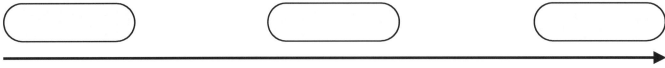

weakly ionising   very strongly ionising

---

4. The properties of radiation are important when we look at how radioactive sources are used.

One use of radioactive sources is in smoke detectors. A diagram of a smoke detector is shown below.

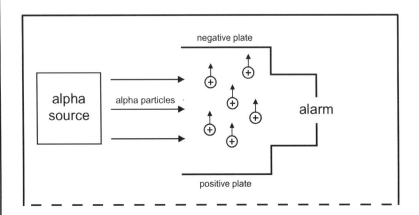

Smoke detectors contain a source of alpha radiation. In normal use, the alpha particles produce ions in the air. The ions are attracted to a negatively-charged metal plate. This generates an electrical current.

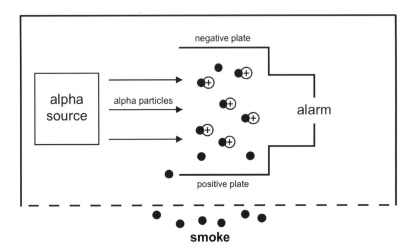

If smoke is present, the smoke particles attach to the ions and prevent them from moving. The electrical current now falls. This is detected by the alarm circuit, which activates the alarm.

a. The outer casing is made from plastic. Suggest why alpha radiation is used rather than beta or gamma.

b. The smoke detector works because alpha radiation generates ions in the air. Suggest why beta or gamma radiation would be less effective.

Nuclear Equations

Exam tip: Although nuclear equations can seem tricky, they are easier than they look. Practising lots of examples will help you to get them.

1. An alpha particle is the same as the nucleus of a helium atom.

The symbol for an alpha particle is shown below.

$$^{4}_{2}\text{He}$$

(protons_____)   (neutrons_____)

a. Complete the diagram to show the number of protons and neutrons in an alpha particle.

b. The equation below shows the alpha decay of an isotope of Uranium.

$$^{238}_{92}\text{U} \longrightarrow ^{234}_{90}\text{Th} + ^{4}_{2}\text{He}$$

Uranium   Thorium

Describe what happens to the atomic number and the mass number during alpha decay.

(During alpha decay, the atomic number _____)

(During alpha decay, the mass number _____)

c. An isotope of radon undergoes alpha decay, producing the element polonium. This is shown below.

$$^{198}_{86}\text{Rn} \longrightarrow \underline{}\text{Po} + ^{4}_{2}\text{He}$$

Radon   Polonium

Complete the equation to show the atomic number and mass number of the polonium isotope produced.

d. An isotope of actinium undergoes alpha decay, producing the element francium. This is shown below.

$$\underline{}\text{Ac} \longrightarrow ^{223}_{87}\text{Fr} + ^{4}_{2}\text{He}$$

Actinium   Francium

Complete the equation to show the atomic number and mass number of the original actinium isotope.

2. As well as alpha decay, elements can also carry out beta decay.

The equation below shows the beta decay of an isotope of radium.

$$^{228}_{88}\text{Ra} \longrightarrow {}^{228}_{89}\text{Ac} + {}^{0}_{-1}e$$

Radium   Actinium

a. Complete the sentences below by selecting the correct words from the boxes.

During beta decay, the atomic number
| increases by 1 |
| decreases by 1 |
| does not change |
but the mass number
| increases by 1 |
| decreases by 1 |
| does not change |
.

This is because a
| nucleus |
| neutron |
| proton |
changes into a proton and an electron (which forms the beta particle).

b. The equation below shows the beta decay of an isotope of lead.

$$^{212}_{82}\text{Pb} \longrightarrow \underline{}\text{Bi} + {}^{0}_{-1}e$$

Lead   Bismuth

Complete the equation to show the atomic number and mass number of the bismuth isotope produced.

c. The equation below shows the beta decay of an isotope of protactinium.

$$\underline{}\text{Pa} \longrightarrow {}^{233}_{92}\text{U} + {}^{0}_{-1}e$$

Protactinium   Uranium

Complete the equation to show the atomic number and mass number of the original protactinium isotope.

3. State which types of radioactive decay are shown in the examples below.

$$^{217}_{85}\text{At} \longrightarrow {}^{213}_{83}\text{Bi} + \boxed{}$$

$$^{208}_{81}\text{Tl} \longrightarrow {}^{208}_{82}\text{Pb} + \boxed{}$$

Exam tip: Remember that in gamma decay, the atomic number
and mass number do not change.

Half-Life

1. Complete the following paragraph using the words below.

| **halve** | **random** | **half-life** | **count rate** | **nucleus** |

Radioactive decay is a _____ process. Scientists cannot predict when any_____

will decay. Instead, scientists measure the_____. This is the time it takes for the number of

undecayed nuclei in a sample to _____. The half-life is also the time taken for the

_____ to fall to half its original level.

2. The graphs below show the decay of two different radioactive isotopes.

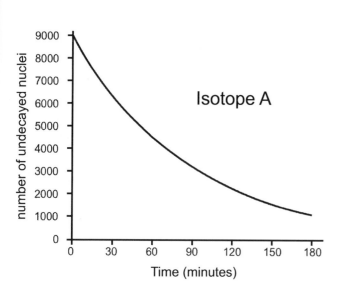

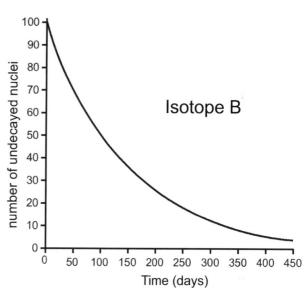

a. Use the graphs to determine the half-lives of the two isotopes.

> Isotope A half-life =
> ....

> Isotope B half-life =
> ....

b. Predict the number of undecayed nuclei of isotope A after 240 minutes.

3. An isotope has a half-life of 3 hours and an initial count rate of 400 counts per second. Calculate the count rate after 12 hours.

4. The alpha-emitter used in smoke detectors has a half-life of 432 years. If the initial count rate is 120 counts per second, calculate the time required for this to fall to 15 counts per second.

Irradiation and Contamination

Exam tip: Many students get confused with the differences between irradiation and contamination. Make sure that you are clear on the differences between these.

1. The diagram below shows a medical syringe being sterilised by irradiation with gamma rays.

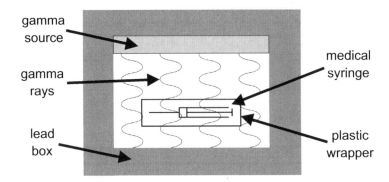

a. The syringe is sealed inside a plastic wrapper. What is the purpose of this?

b. Tick one box to show the advantage of using irradiation to sterilise equipment compared to sterilisation by heating.

Irradiation kills more microbes than heating ☐

Some equipment is damaged by heating ☐

Heating is slower than irradiation ☐

c. Explain why the syringe does not become radioactive after it has been irradiated.

d. Why is it important that medical workers are not exposed to gamma radiation from the steriliser?

e. Medical workers who use beta or gamma radiation often wear lead aprons. Explain why these are not required when working with alpha radiation.

2. In 2011, a tsunami flooded the east coast of Japan. This caused a nuclear power plant to explode.

Large amounts of radioactive isotopes were released into the sea and the surrounding countryside.

a. Select the correct words from the box to complete the sentence.

> **irradiated only**   **contaminated only**   **both irradiated and contaminated**

Crops and fish near the nuclear power plant were _____

b. Workers were sent to the area to help with the clean-up. These were given plastic suits to cover their clothes.

They also wore radiation monitors.

Explain the purpose of the radiation monitors.

c. A student said "Plastic suits protect the workers from both irradiation and contamination".

To what extent do you agree with this statement?

d. Tick the correct boxes to show whether each statement applies to alpha, beta or gamma radiation.

Type of radiation	Alpha	Beta	Gamma
The most ionising radiation			
This radiation can pass through the skin and damage cells			
This radiation is most likely to pass straight through the body			
This radiation is most dangerous when inhaled or swallowed			
This radiation is least ionising			

3. Many studies have been carried out on the effects of radiation on humans.

These studies are published for other scientists to read.

a. What name do scientists give to this process?

b. Why is it important that results are shared with other scientists in this way?

Background Radiation

1. What is meant by background radiation?

2. There are four main sources of background radiation. Two are natural sources and two are man-made.

The four sources of background radiation are shown below.

Draw lines to show whether the sources are natural or man-made.

Accidents at nuclear power stations

Cosmic radiation from space

Natural sources of background radiation

Artificial sources of background radiation

Radioactive elements in rocks

Fallout from nuclear weapons tests

3. A scientist used a Geiger-Muller tube to measure the count rate from background radiation.

Over the course of one minute, the tube counted a total of 180 decays.

The scientist then placed the Geiger-Muller tube near a radioactive source. The count rate was 27 counts per second.

Calculate the count rate that was due only to the radioactive source.

4. The unit of radiation dose is the sievert (Sv).

One sievert is a very large dose of radiation so scientists usually use the millisievert (mSv).

a. The annual average radiation dose in the UK is 2.7 mSv. However, in Cornwall, the average dose is 6.9 mSv.

Suggest why the dose in Cornwall is so much higher than the rest of the UK.

b. During a transatlantic flight, a person can receive a background radiation dose of 0.08 mSv. Suggest why this level of background radiation is much greater than the level experienced by a person on the Earth's surface.

Nuclear Radiation in Medicine

1. Radioactive isotopes are often used as tracers in medicine.

a. What are radioactive tracers used for in medicine? Circle the correct answers.

Radioactive tracers allow doctors to see if a cancer has developed

Radioactive tracers can be used to destroy cancer cells

Radioactive tracers can be used to see if organs are functioning normally

b. Alpha emitters are never used as tracers in the body. Explain why not.

c. Most radioactive tracers used in medicine emit gamma radiation.

Give two reasons why gamma emitters make better tracers than beta emitters.

d. The isotope technetium-99 is often used as a radioactive tracer in medicine. Technetium-99 decays by gamma emission and has a half-life of around 6 hours.

A patient is injected with a sample of technetium-99.

Calculate the fraction of undecayed technetium-99 present in their body after two days.

e. Select the correct word from the box to complete the sentence below.

Radioactive tracers must not decay into

stable
radioactive
different

isotopes. This is because they will continue to

decay, producing ionising radiation and damaging the patient's healthy cells.

2. Ionising radiation can also be used to destroy cancer cells. This is called radiotherapy.

a. State one advantage and one disadvantage of using gamma rays for radiotherapy.

Advantage

Disadvantage

b. In some forms of radiotherapy, the radioactive source is placed inside the patient's body.

Suggest a benefit of this.

Nuclear Fission and Nuclear Fusion

1. Complete the following paragraph using the words below. You will not need all of the words.

hydrogen   **splits**   **uranium**   **stable**   **plutonium**   **unstable**

Nuclear fission takes place with the elements_____ and_____. The nuclei of

these elements are_____. When the nuclei of these elements absorb a neutron, the

nucleus_____.

2. The diagram below shows a Uranium nucleus undergoing nuclear fission.

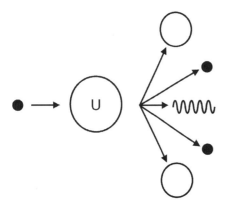

a. Label the diagram with the following labels: daughter nucleus, neutron, radiation.

b. Complete the diagram to show how this process can result in the fission of two more Uranium nuclei.

c. Explain how the diagram above shows a chain reaction.

3. The equation below shows nuclear fission of an isotope of uranium.

$$^{235}_{92}U + n \longrightarrow ^{141}_{56}Ba + ^{92}_{36}Kr + \underline{\quad}n$$

Uranium   neutron   Barium   Strontium   neutrons

a. Complete the diagram to show the number of neutrons released.

b. Calculate the number of atoms of uranium that will have split after five rounds of fission.

In this case, assume that 2 neutrons are released every time a nucleus splits.

4. The diagram below shows a nuclear reactor. These are used to generate electricity.

The nuclear reactor contains fuel rods of uranium or plutonium. These undergo a fission chain reaction.

The fission reaction generates heat which passes into a heat-exchanger.

In the heat-exchanger, water is boiled, producing steam. The steam turns a turbine, generating electricity.

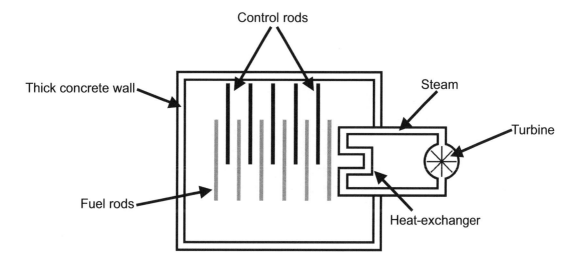

a. When too much heat is released by the chain reaction, control rods are lowered into the reactor.

The control rods are made of a material which absorbs neutrons.

Explain why the rate of the nuclear fission chain reaction slows down when the control rods are lowered into the reactor.

b. Explain why the walls of the nuclear reactor are made of very thick concrete.

c. A nuclear reactor is an example of a controlled chain reaction. Give an example of an uncontrolled chain reaction.

5. In nuclear fusion, light nuclei are fused (joined) to produce a heavier nucleus and release energy.

The diagram on the right shows nuclear fusion.

Explain why nuclear fusion is not an example of a chain reaction.

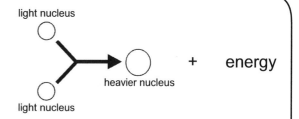

Physics Paper 1

GCSE Specimen Paper

Time allowed: 105 minutes

Maximum marks: 100

Please note that this is a specimen exam paper written by freesciencelessons. The questions are meant to reflect the style of questions that you might see in your GCSE Physics exam.

Neither the exam paper nor the mark scheme have been endorsed by any exam board. The answers are my best estimates of what would be accepted but I cannot guarantee that this would be the case. I do not offer any guarantee that the level you achieve in this specimen paper is the level that you will achieve in the real exam.

1   One of the major uses of energy in the UK is to heat houses.

1 . 1   Thermal energy can pass out of a house through the walls. We can reduce this by packing the walls with insulating material. This is shown in **figure 1**.

Figure 1

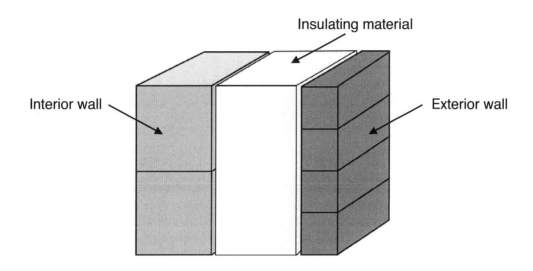

Complete the sentences.

3 marks

The higher the thermal conductivity of a material, the higher the rate of energy

transfer by _____ across the material.

We can reduce thermal energy transfer out of a house by using a material with

a _____ thermal conductivity.

Another way that we can reduce thermal energy transfer out of a house is by

increasing the _____ of the walls.

1 . 2   A student wanted to investigate the thermal conductivity of different types of insulating material. The student used a beaker containing hot water.

The insulating materials were cotton wool, polystyrene beads and bubble wrap.

Describe how the student could carry out this investigation. In your description, you should discuss the different variables involved.

6 marks

1 . 3   In the experiment, the student used a thermometer to measure the temperature of the water.

Figure 2 shows the student reading the thermometer.

Figure 2

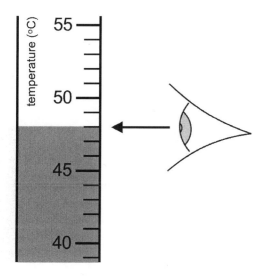

State the resolution of the thermometer.

1 mark

_____

1 . 4   Using a thermometer can lead to errors in the experiment.

Which type of error can be produced when using a thermometer?

Circle one answer.

2 marks

Human error   **Systematic error**   **Random error**

Explain your answer.

_____

_____

_____

Total = 12

2   This question is about domestic electricity in the United Kingdom.

2.1   In the UK, domestic appliances are connected using three-core cable. Three-core cable contains three different colours of wire.

Draw one line from each colour to the correct wire.

3 marks

Blue wire	Earth wire
Brown wire	Neutral wire
Green and yellow striped wire	Live wire

2.2   Appliances such as washing machines have a metal case. If a fault develops, the metal case could carry an electrical current. This could be fatal if someone touched the case.

The following system is designed to prevent this:

• The metal case is connected to the Earth wire.

• The live wire is connected to the electrical supply via a fuse.

Explain how this protects users from a fatal electrical shock.

4 marks

_____

_____

_____

_____

_____

_____

_____

2 . 3   Electricity is transmitted as an alternating current (ac).

Describe the difference between alternating current (ac) and direct current (dc).

2 marks

_____

_____

_____

2 . 4   Electricity is transmitted in the UK via the National Grid.

Which of the following are parts of the National Grid?

Tick **two** boxes only.

2 marks

Houses and factories ☐

Transformers ☐

High-voltage cables ☐

Power stations ☐

2 . 5   The electrical supply is transmitted over the National Grid at a very high voltage.

Explain the advantage of transmitting electricity at a very high voltage.

2 marks

_____

_____

_____

_____

_____

Total = 13

3 A scientist took a sample of solid chemical. They gently heated the chemical and measured the temperature every minute.

The scientist plotted the results on a graph. This is shown in **figure 3**.

Figure 3

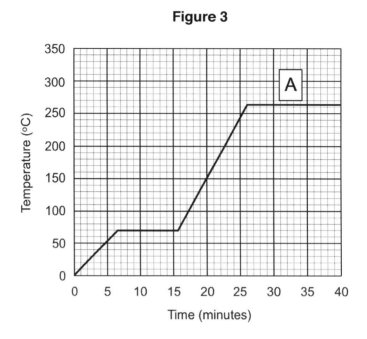

3 . 1 Give the name of the change of state taking place at part A on the graph.

1 mark

_____

3 . 2 Use the graph to determine the melting point of the substance.

1 mark

_____

3 . 3 The specific latent heat of fusion of the chemical is 180 000 J / kg.

Calculate the energy required to melt 0.5 kg of the chemical.

(You will need to select the correct equation from the equation sheet).

2 marks

_____

_____

_____

_____

Energy = _____ J

3 . 4   When we heat any substance, we increase its internal energy.

What is meant by internal energy?

2 marks

_____

_____

_____

_____

3 . 5   Explain why the temperature of a substance does not change when the substance is melting or boiling.

1 mark

_____

_____

_____

3 . 6   A scientist was testing a different chemical. They heated 300 g of the chemical. The temperature increased from 25°C to 130°C.

The specific heat capacity of the chemical was 2150 J/kg °C.

Calculate the change in thermal energy required to heat the chemical.

(You will need to select the correct equation from the equation sheet).

3 marks

_____

_____

_____

_____

_____

_____

_____

Energy = _____ J

Total = 10

4   A teacher was investigating radioactive decay. The apparatus that they used is shown in **figure 4**.

Figure 4

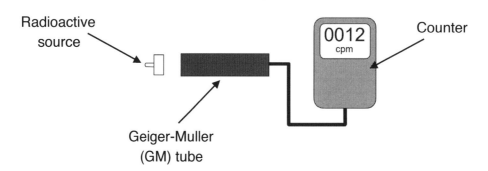

Radioactive source

0012 cpm

Counter

Geiger-Muller (GM) tube

4 . 1   The source contains a radioactive isotope.

What is meant by an isotope?

2 marks

_____

_____

_____

4 . 2   The teacher placed different materials between the radioactive source and the GM tube. For each material, the teacher measured the count-rate detected by the GM tube.

The teacher's results are shown in **table 1**.

Table 1

Material	Count rate (counts per minute)
No material	240
A sheet of paper	240
3 mm of aluminium	63

Explain how the results show that the source was not emitting alpha radiation.

1 mark

_____

_____

4.3 When no material was placed between the radioactive source and the GM tube, the count rate was 240 counts per minute.

The level of background radiation was 0.2 counts per second.

Calculate the count rate due only to the radioactive source.

3 marks

_____

_____

_____

_____

Count rate due only to radioactive source = _____ counts per second

4.4 State one natural and one man-made source of background radiation.

2 marks

Natural source   _____

_____

Man-made source   _____

_____

4.5 The teacher concluded that the source was emitting beta particles.

Describe how a beta particle is formed.

3 marks

_____

_____

_____

_____

_____

Total = 11

5   A student set up an electrical circuit containing two resistors in series. The circuit is shown in **figure 5**.

Figure 5

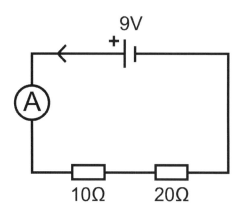

5.1   What is the potential difference across the two resistors.

2 marks

Potential difference across 10Ω resistor = _____ V

Potential difference across 20Ω resistor = _____ V

5.2   Calculate the current in the above circuit.

3 marks

_____

_____

_____

Current = _____ A

5.3   The student changed the circuit, placing the resistors in parallel.

How would the current change? Give a reason for your answer.

2 marks

_____

_____

_____

5.4   The student set up a different circuit. This is shown in **figure 6**.

Figure 6

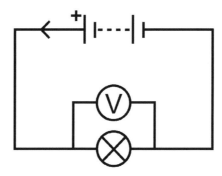

0.5 C of charge flowed through the filament lamp. The potential difference across the filament lamp was 9V.

Calculate the energy transferred by the filament lamp.

3 marks

Energy transferred = _____ J

5.5   The student reversed the direction of one of the cells.

What would happen to the filament lamp? Assume that both cells have a potential difference of 4.5 V.

Give a reason for your answer.

2 marks

_____

_____

_____

_____

Question 5 continues on the next page.

5.6   Sketch the current - potential difference graph for a filament lamp on the axes below.

current

1 mark

potential
difference

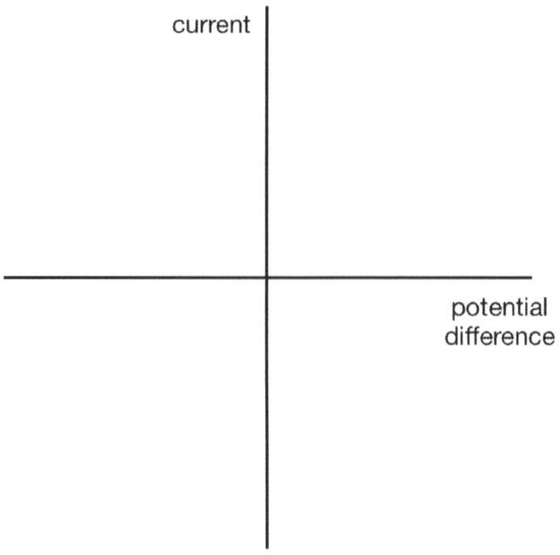

5.7   Explain why a filament lamp is a non-ohmic conductor.

3 marks

_____

_____

_____

_____

_____

_____

_____

_____

5.8   The student decided to replace the filament lamp with a light-emitting diode (LED).

Circle the correct symbol for a light-emitting diode below.

1 mark

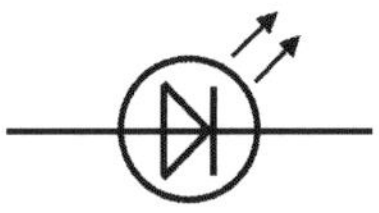

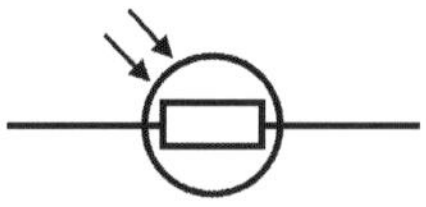

5.9   Describe one advantage of using an LED compared to a filament lamp.

1 mark

_____

_____

Total = 18

6   An electric motor was used to lift a 5 kg mass. This is shown in **figure 7**.

Figure 7

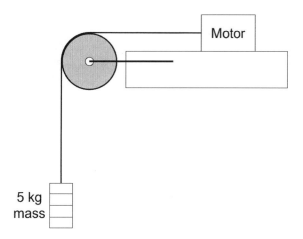

6 . 1   The mass was lifted to a height of 30 cm.

Calculate the change in the gravitational potential energy store of the mass.

The value of g is 9.8 N / kg   **3 marks**

_____

_____

_____

                Change in gravitational potential energy store = _____ J

6 . 2   The motor continued lifting the mass until the total change in gravitational potential energy was 30 J.

The motor was switched on for 5 minutes. Calculate the power of the motor.

You should include the unit for power.

                                                                   3 marks

_____

_____

_____

                                        Power = _____

6 . 3   The motor was used to lift a different mass. The change in the gravitational potential energy store of the mass was 150 J.

A total of 200 J of energy was transferred by the motor.

Calculate the efficiency of the motor.

2 marks

_____

_____

_____

Efficiency = _____

6 . 4   Electricity can be generated by burning fossil fuels. Fossil fuels are a non-renewable resource.

What is meant by non-renewable.

1 mark

_____

_____

6 . 5   Apart from being non-renewable, describe another disadvantage of burning fossil fuels to generate electricity.

2 marks

_____

_____

_____

Total = 11

7   Plutonium undergoes radioactive decay. The nuclear equation for this is shown below.

$$^{238}_{94}\text{Pu} \longrightarrow {}^{\cdots}_{\cdots}\text{U} + {}^{4}_{2}\text{He}$$

7.1   Complete the equation to show the mass number and atomic number of the daughter element.

2 marks

7.2   Which type of radioactive decay is shown by the equation?

Give a reason for your answer.

2 marks

_____

_____

_____

7.3   When handling radioactive isotopes, scientists must wear protection against irradiation and contamination.

Describe what is meant by irradiation and contamination.

2 marks

_____

_____

_____

_____

_____

_____

Question 7 continues on the next page.

7.4 Scientists can determine the half-life for different radioactive isotopes.

What is meant by half-life?

1 mark

_____

_____

_____

7.5 **Figure 8** shows the number of undecayed nuclei of plutonium-238 at different times.

Figure 8

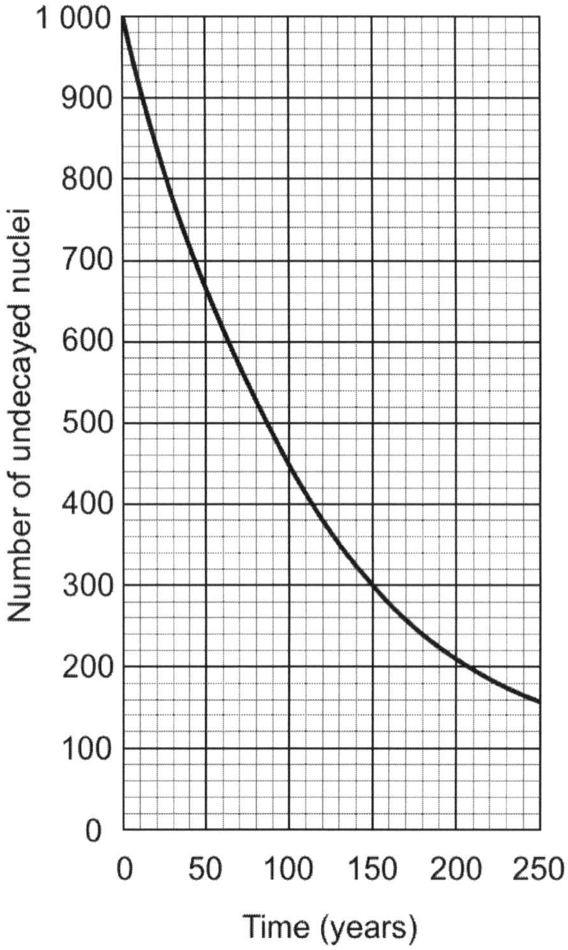

Use figure 8 to determine the half-life of plutonium-238.

1 mark

Half-life = _____ years

7 . 6   Certain isotopes of plutonium undergo nuclear fission.

This is used to generate electricity in nuclear reactors.

Describe the process of nuclear fission taking place in nuclear reactors.

5 marks

_____

_____

_____

_____

_____

_____

7 . 7   Nuclear fission in a nuclear reactor is a controlled process.

State an example of uncontrolled nuclear fission.

1 mark

_____

7 . 8   Nuclear fusion takes place in stars.

Describe what happens in nuclear fusion.

2 marks

_____

_____

_____

_____

Total = 16

8   This question is about density.

8.1   **Figure 9** shows a block of metal.

Figure 9

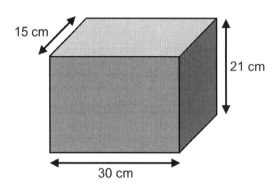

The mass of the block is 50 kg. Determine the density of the metal.

Express your answer to 4 significant figures.

3 marks

_____

_____

_____

Density = _____ kg / m³

8.2   Describe how you would carry out an experiment to determine the density of an irregular-shaped object.

6 marks

_____

_____

_____

_____

_____

You may continue your answer on the following page.

Total = 9

End of questions

Printed in Great Britain
by Amazon

40760198R00075